Knowing Christ

Also by Alister McGrath

In the Beginning
The Journey
Theology for Amateurs
To Know and Serve God
Why Does God Allow Suffering?

Knowing Christ

Alister McGrath

Hodder & Stoughton
LONDON SYDNEY AUCKLAND

Copyright © 2001 by Alister McGrath

First published in Great Britain in 2001

The right of Alister McGrath to be identified as the Author of
the Work has been asserted by him in accordance with the
Copyright, Designs and Patents Act 1988.

10 9 8 7 6 5 4 3

British Library Cataloguing in Publication Data
A record for this book is available from the British Library

ISBN 0 340 75678 0

Typeset by Avon Dataset Ltd, Bidford-on-Avon, Warks

Printed and bound in Great Britain by
The Guernsey Press Co. Ltd, Channel Islands

Hodder & Stoughton
A Division of Hodder Headline Ltd
338 Euston Road
London NW1 3BH

Contents

Introduction

'I regard everything as loss because of the surpassing value of knowing Christ Jesus my Lord' (Philippians 3:8). Every now and then, we encounter words that electrify us. I can still remember the first time I stumbled across those words of Paul, written to the church at Philippi. I read them about eighteen months after I had begun my life as a Christian. It was May 1973, and I was a mere twenty years old, in the second year of my studies at Oxford University. I decided to get up very early – not something that comes easily or naturally to students – and cycle out to Wytham Woods, some distance from the centre of Oxford. It was a glorious late spring morning. As it was a Sunday, there was little traffic on the roads. I arrived at the outskirts of the woods and climbed a grassy knoll. There, in front of me, were the dreaming spires of Oxford, surrounded by the sheen of an early morning mist. It was an awesome experience.

I spent perhaps fifteen minutes enjoying the scene. I then turned to read Paul's letter to the Philippians from beginning to end in one session – something I had never done before. I cannot recall why I chose to read this letter. Perhaps some kind and well-meaning friend had recommended it. I found myself pausing at point after point, trying to take in Paul's reflections on the unsearchable riches of Christ. 'For to me, living is Christ, and dying is gain' (Philippians 1:21). That certainly pulled me up. For Paul, the entire purpose of life was Christ. And death was to be *welcomed* as something that brought him closer to the Christ he loved, and who in turn loved him so much. I began to feel a deep sense of longing. I wanted to know Christ like that. Then I encountered that statement in the third chapter: 'I regard everything as loss because of the surpassing value of knowing Christ Jesus my Lord.'

I am not normally an ambitious person. I don't regard this as making any especial claim to virtue. It's probably just that I lack the drive that makes other people want to achieve great things. But I felt a sense of ambition that morning. I wanted to share Paul's conviction that nothing in the whole world compared to knowing Christ. I thought long and hard about Paul's words. It was if he was speaking to me, and me alone. He was asking me if I shared his certainty that the privilege of knowing Christ overshadowed everything and anything else that this world had to offer. And as I looked at the spires of Oxford, now bathed in a gentle sunlight after the mist had been burned away, I knew what the answer to that question was.

No, I did not. But one day, I would.

Why were those words so important to me? Why were they so significant on that May morning? I need to tell a little of my own story at this point, to bring out the weakness they had so powerfully exposed.

One of the childhood experiences which I recall most vividly is lying awake on my bed at night, looking out of a window towards the stars in the night sky. I was then aged about fourteen, and was fairly sure that I knew everything that mattered and had all the great issues of life sorted out. Back in the 1960s, most young people seemed to assume that religion was a waste of time. Marxism was much more attractive – and relevant! I was going to be a research scientist and sort out the problems of the world through new cures for diseases. During my final years at the Methodist College, Belfast, I concentrated on the natural sciences, intending to study these in more detail when I went on to university.

I still regarded myself as a Marxist at this stage, although subtle doubts had begun to creep in. Yet the certainties on which my life was grounded were slowly being eroded. One of the issues which troubled me was the question of mortality. What was the point of life? It seemed so brief and insignificant. Looking at the stars increased my sense of despondency. I knew that some of the stars I was observing were so far away that their light took hundreds of years to reach me. This meant that I would be dead before the light now being emitted by those stars would reach the earth. I found it a disturbing thought, partly because I had no real answer to the issues it raised. More fundamentally, however, it threatened to open a Pandora's box, from which would emerge all kinds of ideas that would disturb the neatly arranged furniture of what I hoped was my settled Marxist worldview. I had systematically excluded religion from my philosophy, arguing that it was a human construction fabricated to shield individuals against the harsh realities of life. While this now sounds absurd, I must point out that it was a widespread perception in the 1960s, shored up by the authority of Marx and Lenin.

The classic way of dealing with such awkward thoughts is, of course, to ignore them and hope that they will go away. Yet this particular thought, and an increasing number of distant cousins, obstinately refused to do anything of the sort. Although I was not aware of this, I was heading towards what Thomas Kuhn encourages us to call a 'paradigm shift' – a major change in the way we see and think about reality. Or, to use the more traditional and helpful language of the Christian tradition, I was about to get converted.

My discovery of the Christian faith took place in October or November 1971, when I was eighteen, shortly after I arrived at Oxford University to study the natural sciences. Looking back on that time of my life, it is clear that my early rejection of Christianity was based on a misunderstanding. My outlook on life up to that point had been shaped by my reactions to what I can now see was a caricature of religion. Perhaps that caricature was ideally suited to the needs of a schoolboy who wanted quick answers to complex questions. The doubts I had tried to suppress about the credibility of my Marxist outlook began to resurface. Like Augustine in the cathedral at Milan, I would attend Christian meetings in my attempt to discover what it was all about. Oxford University offered me the freedom, space and time to think about life more critically than before, and I came to the conclusion that I had misjudged and misunderstood Christianity. It had something to offer – something which I knew I had not fully grasped, yet which seemed more intellectually resilient and attractive than its many rivals. Aware that Christianity was taking hold of me, I chose to take hold of it in turn. Without wishing to sound pious, that transitional period in late 1971 was of formative importance to the rest of my life.

It would be foolish and quite inaccurate to say that my conversion sorted everything out. In one sense, it opened a door on a new set of questions, many of which I was poorly equipped to answer. Conversion is perhaps one of the most unsettling experiences of life. All of my certainties had been swept away, and I had to begin thinking all over again. Old questions needed new answers. In addition, I now had to wrestle with questions which had never troubled me before. How can the existence of a loving God be reconciled with the existence of sin in the world? Or, perhaps a little less abstractly and more urgently, what should I do with the rest of my life?

Faced with new questions, it is fatally easy to provide quick and easy answers – answers which may offer temporary fixes, but which are quite inadequate as long-term solutions. Like so many Christians in the first stages of their spiritual development, I found myself occasionally puzzled and sometimes more than a little distressed by some of the answers provided by well-meaning

Christian friends, who often seemed to know as little about their faith as I did. Some of the visiting speakers at the university Christian Union seemed to think that the hallmark of Christian maturity was a point-blank refusal to think about their faith. We were asked to trust the speakers, and that seemed to be about as far as it went.

I do not think that I was ever tempted to give up my new-found faith on account of the shallowness of some of these presentations. Nevertheless, I was quite convinced that there had to be more intellectual substance to the Christian faith than I had found in student Christianity. I regularly found myself sneaking home to read C. S. Lewis, whose discussions of difficult issues seemed incalculably more satisfactory than those offered elsewhere.

I do not mean to be totally negative about those who offer such quick fixes to Christian students. These students are often at a very early stage in their Christian lives and need a lot of patience, care and love. Nor am I dismissing out of hand their demand to accept their ideas as truth, rather than to think about it. It is, however, fair to point out that many of these young lives of faith will later become shipwrecked on the rocks of precisely those questions to which inadequate answers have been given – after they have been discouraged from seeking better ones out of some misguided belief that this reflects a lack of trust in God.

It became clear to me that I wanted – and needed – to study the Christian faith in depth. This irritated the 'don't think – trust!' people, something which did not trouble me as much as it probably should have. As someone who was studying the natural sciences, I was particularly interested in thinking more deeply about the relation of Christianity and my own subject. Nevertheless, it had become clear to me that there was another need that I was increasingly aware of – the need to *explain* the ideas of Christianity. Young Christians – and here I had my own experience in mind as much as anything – needed to be reassured that the leading ideas of the Christian faith made sense; that they rested on secure foundations; and that the Christian faith would be impoverished and compromised if they were not here. In short, I became aware of the need for the explanation, justification and appreciation of Christian teachings.

Yet alongside a growing awareness of the wonderful coherence of Christianity, I was becoming aware of a spiritual chasm opening up. It was as if my mind and heart were being pulled in different directions. I began to notice that my 'knowledge' of the Christian faith was rather dry and cerebral. There seemed to be two totally different things going on in my life, and they did not connect up. What I thought and what I experienced seemed like separate insulated compartments within me which never communicated with each other. Which should I trust? And on which should I build my house of faith?

Part of the difficulty was that I was, like most people of my generation, deeply influenced by the notion that Christianity was basically about *ideas*. This wasn't really my fault. I had grown up within a western culture which was still shaped by the ideas of the Enlightenment – the great cultural movement, whose origins lay in the eighteenth century, which demanded that human reason should determine and judge all things. This was the intellectual air I breathed, without realising that I was buying into a seriously deficient view of life and faith.

The impact was considerable. Theological correctness became something of an obsession with me, as it was for many Christian students of the 1970s. The important thing was to get our ideas right, often by learning sections of works of systematic theology. What I failed to realise was that the gospel affects every level of our existence – not just the way we think, but the way in which we *feel* and *live*. The Enlightenment had championed the role of reason and vetoed any engagement with emotions or imagination. Many influential English pastors, unable to break free of their 'stiff upper lip' mentality, doubtless inherited from their days at England's top public schools, looked down their noses at any kind of engagement with the emotions. A faith that affected the emotions was dismissed as a ridiculous idea, like having women prime ministers or wanting to get married.

Yet I knew that writers such as C. S. Lewis had stressed the importance of precisely those aspects of our Christian lives which were being ridiculed by those who should have known better. I gradually came to the realisation that my faith was far too academic. Frankly, it was as dry as dust. I was spiritually parched, and the last thing I needed was more of the dry and desiccated material that seemed to be the staple diet of so many at this time. I needed refreshment and a rekindling of my vision of the gospel. I wanted to be excited by my faith, to be set on fire with a new love for Christ. What I got were sermons and talks offering detailed exegesis of a few biblical verses, which somehow never quite seemed to make the connection between the text and real life.

Sermons at Oxford churches with large student congregations seemed to stress the importance of knowing the Bible rather than knowing Christ. Advancing biblical knowledge was seen as an end in itself, with students being encouraged to memorise proof texts. The cultivation of an intimate personal relationship with Christ somehow seemed to be marginalised. 'Know your Bible' seemed to be the supreme goal of these churches. They certainly produced students who knew their Bible well. Yet, sadly, many of those who could quote the most obscure biblical verses in support of some tenuous theological argument had never known the tender embrace of a loving Christ and nestled in his care. A means had become an end. The text which was meant to lead us to Christ and allow him to convert and renew us had become a goal in its own right. Knowledge of a text had displaced knowledge of Christ. It was a dangerous and deplorable situation which could well lead to a weak and vulnerable faith, inadequately rooted in a personal relationship with the living Christ.

I fully concede the need to get our ideas right, and the supreme importance of Scripture in determining and shaping

Christian doctrines. Yet doctrines are like a framework, ensuring that the living presence of Christ is understood correctly. They allow us to avoid thinking in vague or mystical terms about Christ, helping us to understand more about the living personal presence of Christ within us. Yet so often, Oxford students like me seemed to have a framework without a presence, ideas without a person. It was as if the framework constructed to secure the living presence of Christ within the soul of the believer was in place – but it contained nothing. The cage was there – but there was no living, roaring lion within it.

Thoughts like this were racing round in my mind as I mulled over Paul's words on that May morning back in 1973. 'I count everything as loss because of the surpassing worth of knowing Christ Jesus my Lord.' I knew that there was something contained or conveyed within those words that I had yet to discover. Perhaps I had an inkling of what he was talking about – but the fulness of his meaning had thus far eluded me. And so I made my decision. I was going to try and find out what he meant, and do something about it.

This proved far harder than I had thought. I suppose I had expected that I would just pick up a few useful ideas about how to pray better, or get more out of reading a biblical passage. What happened was actually rather different. I found that I was challenged as much as I was affirmed. I was forced to face up to my own weaknesses and pride. I found that I was broken down before I was built up again. It was as if a mirror was being held up to me, to help me realise my own weaknesses and frailty. I was being invited to set out on a voyage of discovery. I thought that I would find out more about Christ. Yet I ended up discovering more about myself, and realising how much I needed to change. This little book is an attempt to put into words some of the lessons I learned, often painfully, as I wrestled with what it meant to know Christ and to see this as the greatest privilege we can hope to be granted.

In the end, the answer to my questions and prayers came

about many years later, in a quite unexpected way. As an academic, I had been asked to teach a class at Oxford dealing with Christian spirituality from 1000 to 1600. This class would survey the approaches to Christian spirituality that had been developed during the Middle Ages and the period of the Reformation. It was not a subject I knew very much about at that stage. So I did what any responsible teacher would be expected to do: I immersed myself in the devotional writings of people like Bernard of Cluny, Anselm of Canterbury, Martin Luther, John Calvin and Ignatius Loyola. My main aim in doing this was to equip myself to teach others about Christian spirituality. Yet, in one of those great paradoxes of grace, I found that I – who was meant to be the teacher! – was actually *being taught*.

I now realise that one of the ways in which God invites us to develop in our Christian lives is to listen to older and wiser voices, allowing their maturity to temper the enthusiasm of a young faith. I began to take notes on what I encountered in these texts that I found helpful, stimulating, encouraging or challenging. It did not take long for me to realise that I had stumbled by accident upon a technique which had long been known to others. Thus the noted French spiritual writer Francis de Sales (1567–1622) uses the image of gathering flowers from a garden to illustrate exactly this point in his *Introduction to the Devout Life* (1609):

Those who have been walking in a beautiful garden do not leave it willingly without taking away with them in their hands four or five flowers, in order to inhale their fragrance and carry them about during the day. Even so, when we have considered some mystery in meditation, we should choose one or two or three points which we have found particularly to our taste, and which are particularly appropriate to our advancement, so that we may remember them during the day, and inhale their fragrance spiritually.[1]

As I read and reflected, I found that the voices from the past that I was studying challenged me at point after point. Had I not realised I had missed out on so much? Should I not try other approaches to knowing Christ than the one I knew so well?

Yes, I knew Christ – but I did not know him to anything like the extent that I could or should. Others seemed to know him far better. It was like being in a vast hall, from which a number of doors led off to rooms beyond. Each room was filled with treasures. My problem was that I thought there was only one door. Foolishly, I believed that what lay beyond was all there was to be known about Christ. The result was inevitable. The quality of my relationship with Christ was impoverished.

It was not that my knowledge of Christ was misguided or that my trust in him was misplaced. It was simply that I assumed that what I knew was all there was to know. Perhaps this is the greatest form of spiritual arrogance – believing that what we know is all that there is to be known. At any rate, this was the situation where I found myself. Without realising what I was doing, I had cut myself off from many of 'the boundless riches of Christ' (Ephesians 3:8). I had amassed information about Christ without knowing him in the warmth and intimacy of a personal relationship.

There are many others who could tell of experiences like this, and who could write more powerfully and eloquently than I ever could. They began the life of faith with enthusiasm and commitment, yet found the vitality of faith becoming eroded with the passage of time. For some, the problem lay in an excessively intellectual approach to their faith – the approach that I once adopted. It was not wrong, just lacking. Others will have become shipwrecked through inadequate ways of knowing Christ. Some rely too much on religious experience and come to place their trust in the way they feel about Christ. While wishing to know Christ, they end up depending upon their own personal subjective worlds. Others feel a deep personal loyalty to Christ, perhaps through the witness of friends and family – but have never allowed loyalty to be transformed into the intimacy of a personal relationship. They are missing out on one of the most precious gifts that God offers to his people – the living presence of Christ in their lives.

They say that the lessons you learn best are the ones that are the hardest to learn. Well, I have learned much over the last twenty-five years, often painfully and usually slowly. I would be thrilled if others could learn from my experience. The mistakes that I made in the early stages of my Christian life could, I think, be gathered together under two broad headings.

1   I failed to appreciate the full implications of Paul's image of the 'body of Christ' (1 Corinthians 12:12–31), which clearly assumes that each Christian must expect to give to, and receive from, others. I tended to think of my faith in very strongly individualist terms, seeing myself as a spiritual Lone Ranger who did not need to receive from others. A breakthrough came when I realised that, by God's grace, I could learn from others, both living and dead. Those who were making the walk of faith around me, and had made it before me, could pass on their insights and wisdom. I began to realise that my belief in my spiritual self-sufficiency was nothing more than a self-deception, which blinded me to the riches that I could gain from listening to others and benefiting from God's work in their lives.

2   I deployed only a fraction of the God-given resources within myself to the task of knowing and loving Christ. The emphasis I inherited, upon using only the human mind when knowing Christ, was not grounded in the New Testament but in the secular and rationalist worldview of the Enlightenment. Through this excessive over-reliance upon the human mind I had become blinded by the 'god of this world', and had failed to behold the full radiance of the glory of the gospel of Christ (2 Corinthians 4:4). I needed

to bring every resource that God had entrusted to me to knowing Christ more fully.

In this book, I have set out to help others learn from my own many mistakes, and to provide access to at least some of the resources and ideas I found so helpful in opening the way to a richer appreciation and deeper experience of the Christian knowledge of Christ. Please treat what follows as an exploration of spiritual possibilities, some of which may work for you and others of which may not. God creates, loves and knows us as individuals, and relates to us in ways that reflect our distinctive identities. Please take up anything that you find useful and discard whatever turns out to be unhelpful. Or, as St Paul has it, 'test everything; hold fast to what is good' (1 Thessalonians 5:21).

ALISTER MCGRATH
Oxford, 2000

PART 1

Where Christ is to be known

How can we know Christ in all his fulness? Paul prayed that his readers might comprehend the full breadth, length, height and depth of Christ (Ephesians 3:18). These are images of spaciousness – images which affirm the vastness of Christ's significance, and which invite us to discover him more fully. We must learn to be dissatisfied with our present apprehension of Christ, and yearn to know and experience more. After all, spaces are meant to be explored and inhabited. Paul here prays that his readers might discover new horizons to their knowledge of Christ, being excited by the new vistas they will see and the fresh opportunities for growth they will be offered.

Paul's imagery is thus profoundly enticing. It encourages us to think of the immensity of this world in which we live, and realise how little of it we know at first hand. We only experience a small part of the world – perhaps the city in which we live, or occasionally more distant parts which we visit on business or vacation. But there is so much more to this world! It awaits our discovery – as does the fulness of Christ. Again, think of the vastness of the starry heavens above us, reaching into the depths of the universe. We may be content with crawling on the face of the earth, but there is more to be discovered and experienced – as there is with Christ.

Or think of the depths of the vast oceans. We may be perfectly content to sit on the shoreline and look out over the face of the sea. Yet beneath its surface lie hidden depths, awaiting our discovery, with a power to amaze and excite us. So it is with Christ. We may rest content with what we know. Yet by not going deeper we risk our faith becoming stale and complacent. We refuse to allow Christ to lead us further and deeper into his arms.

For it is God's will that we should know Christ fully and rejoice in that knowledge. We have been created so that we might know Christ, and will never achieve our God-given potential or goals until we do so. We have been designed by our creator with an inbuilt need and capacity to know him, and we will wander restlessly through life unless we do know him. 'You have made us for yourself, and our heart is restless until it finds its rest in you' (Augustine of Hippo). Everyone wants to find something that is really worthwhile, that will give life meaning, purpose and fulfilment. The search for purpose in life is one of the greatest themes of human existence. Christianity honours this quest. Yet it insists that this hunger for significance can only be satisfied by encountering and knowing Christ.

At first sight, this might move us to despair. If we can only achieve the fulfilment that God longs for us to have through knowing Christ, what hope can we have? I might long to know Christ – *but would he want anything to do with me*? Countless good people have lain awake at night, sleepless, deeply disturbed by this thought. Since the Son of God already knows what I am like, surely he will reject me as unworthy of his company and favour. Yet Christ already knows us, through and through. There is no aspect of our being which is hidden from his gaze. He knows us, exactly as we are. There can be – and need be – no secrets withheld from him. He knows us as we are and loves us, willingly giving his own precious life in order that we might live through him.

The Christ who knows us so well longs for us to know him in turn. So how are we to know him? How can we make sure that we know him for all his worth? In this opening section, I shall explore some ways that I found helpful as I tried to grasp as much as I could of the significance, wonder and power of Christ.

To contemplate Christ is to be confronted with a dramatic and arresting combination of a question mark and an exclamation mark. In Christ, God proclaims to us, in tenderness and anger, 'I will love you!' In Christ, God asks of us, in joy and in pain, 'Will you love me as I love you?' In their various ways, all of the Gospel accounts of the ministry of Christ confront us with that challenging invitation. They leave us to reflect on that question, but clearly expect and await an answer.

Our Lord was once asked which of the commandments was the greatest. His reply is of no small importance to our theme: 'You shall love the Lord your God with all your heart, and with all your soul, and with all your mind' (Matthew 22:37). We are to love God with all of our God-given faculties. Every aspect of our being is to be brought to bear on the duty and joy of loving the God who created and redeemed us. The same is true of knowing Christ.

Christ longs to nourish our minds with his truth; to raise our imaginations to new heights through his beauty; to open our hearts to his love; to surrender our wills to his purpose; and to allow his holiness to challenge the way we behave. In every way, Christ lays the most fundamental challenge to the root of our lives: in all things, he asks us to submit our entire being to his wise and loving rule. To know Christ is to begin this process of change and renewal.

When I began my Christian life, I naturally thought of 'knowing Christ' as a task for my mind. The key to spiritual growth would surely lie in a deepening understanding of who Jesus Christ is and what he achieved through the cross and resurrection. I therefore began my quest for an enhanced understanding of my faith. This brought about some important results, not least of which was that I found myself profoundly reassured concerning the intellectual resilience of the Christian faith.

Yet, as I look back, I can now see that my virtually exclusive focus on the mind led to a form of spiritual impoverishment. Christ is indeed to be known in the mind – but he is also to be known at a far deeper level. I read the Bible as a source of *information*, where others who were wiser than I read it as a source of *formation* – of being shaped and formed by what they read, as they allowed it to impact upon their hearts, minds and emotions. I had yet to discover the ways of reading Scripture in which the mind descends into the heart, as both are drawn into the love and presence of God.

Christian theology makes a distinction between two senses of the word 'faith'. On the one hand, there is the 'faith which believes' – that is, the personal activity of trust and commitment in God. On the other, there is the 'faith which is believed' – that is, the body of Christian doctrine. In my case, the 'faith which is believed' remained unaltered. Yet I realised that my grasp of the totality of the Christian gospel had been shallow. I experienced a deepening in the quality of my faith, rather than any change in what I believed. What developed and matured was the 'faith which believes' – my personal attitude of trust in God. The New Testament often compares the kingdom of God to a growing plant, or a seed taking root. What happened to me was that a plant which had grown to some extent underwent a new spurt of growth, leading to increased strength and vitality.

In what follows, I shall explore my growing awareness of my need to probe deeper into the Christian faith, and consider some of the resources that helped me to discover its depths.

1

Knowing Christ in our minds

God has created us with the gift of understanding, and clearly expects us to use our minds in deepening our grasp of and commitment to the gospel. Knowing Christ is partly about knowing more about Christ – about deepening our understanding of who he is and what he achieved for us.

This is an immensely important theme. Christ demands to be understood. He calls upon us, as he called upon the disciples of old, to tell him and others who we think he is (Mark 8:27). Who is this person who enters into people's lives and so radically transforms them? How can we even begin to offer an explanation of his identity? To grasp who Christ is means appreciating who he is *for us*, and hence to open the door to spiritual growth in and through him. The greatest minds of the Christian Church have addressed this question down the ages, and constantly found themselves failing to do justice to it. There is always more to Christ than we appreciate. All our explanations and theories can do is give us access to part of the truth. What we see is wonderful; what remains to be discovered is likely to be more wonderful still.

There is more to Christ than our minds will ever be able to embrace. Hilary of Poitiers, a Christian writer of the fourth century, expressed this point well when he wrote: 'We are compelled to attempt what is unattainable, to climb where we cannot reach, to speak what we cannot utter. Instead of the bare adoration of faith, we are under an obligation to entrust the deepest matters of faith to human language.'

The Gospel writers set us alongside the disciples as they encounter Jesus for the first time and gradually begin to grasp his significance. He enters into their world as a mysterious figure, someone who commands authority. When the apostles heard his call to follow them, they left everything behind and walked alongside him. They did not fully understand who he was or what he had in mind for them, but there was something about him that was attractive and compelling. Leaving behind all that they counted precious, they walked into the unknown future, knowing that it would include the consolation of his presence. They would spend the remainder of their lives appreciating who Christ is and why he is so important.

As we read the Gospels, we realise that we are being set alongside the apostles on their journey of discovery, seeing and hearing the remarkable events which gradually brought them to the electrifying realisation that here among them was none other than the Son of God. The Gospels allow us to see with the eyes of the first disciples, taking in with them Christ's encounters with those around him. We can hear the astonishing words of Christ with our own ears, and share in the dawn of faith – the moment when they realised that here, in front of their eyes, was the hope of Israel and the one who held their future in his hands.

What they experienced – and what we can experience *through* them – was a series of clues, building up to disclose both the identity of Christ and the meaning of their lives. What they saw were brush strokes, individually applied to the canvas yet collectively disclosing a glorious landscape. What they experienced were individual pieces of a jigsaw puzzle, combining to reveal a pattern, a face – the face of the Son of God, who loves us and gave himself for us. The words and deeds of Jesus flow together, merging and melding to yield a picture of the one who holds the key to life and death, to the riddles and tragedies of our human existence. The greatest puzzle the world has ever known is the identity of Jesus. 'Who do *you* say that I am?' (Mark 8:27–9). To answer this question, we have to put together the many pieces of the New Testament witness to the identity and significance of Jesus and examine the picture they disclose.

So what are these pieces? As I reflected on this question, I found myself trying to lay out on the table of my mind the main themes that I knew had to be incorporated into my understanding of Christ.

First, it was clear to me that the New Testament sees Christ as the fulfilment of the hopes of Israel. As Matthew's Gospel points out so often, Christ is the Messiah, the long-awaited deliverer of God's people. I frequently found myself reading Matthew's account of the birth of Christ (Matthew 1–2) and noting how often the theme of the fulfilment of prophecy is identified as being of importance. However I understood Christ, he had to be seen as part of the long history of a faithful and patient God's relations with his wayward and lost people.

Second, I tried to identify as many as I could of the titles that the New Testament writers use to refer to him, each of which tells us something special about him. He is 'Lord' – the same title used to refer to God in the Old Testament. He is both the 'Son of God' and the 'Son of Man'. Occasionally, he is even referred to explicitly as 'God'. I found myself producing lists of all these titles, and trying to make sense of the immensely complex and rich portrait of Christ that they disclosed. Whatever understanding of Christ I finally arrived at would have to do justice to each of these titles.

One title of Christ that attracted my attention in particular was 'Saviour'. The New Testament regularly speaks of Christ in this way, even in the accounts of Christ's birth. Mary and Joseph were directed to name their child Jesus because he would save his people from their sins (Matthew 1:21). The shepherds in the fields close to Bethlehem learned of the birth of the 'Saviour, who is the Messiah, the Lord' (Luke 2:11). This theme resonates throughout the New Testament. Yet I was aware that only God can save. The Old Testament prophets regularly reminded Israel that she cannot save herself, nor can she be saved by the idols of the nations round about her. It is the Lord, and the Lord alone, who will save her (Isaiah 45:21–2).

I therefore found it exciting and challenging to take in – and try to make sense of – the astonishing fact that, knowing full well that it was God alone who could save, the first Christians had no hesitation in affirming that *Christ* was their Saviour. This was no misunderstanding on the part of people who were ignorant of the Old Testament. It was fundamentally recognition of what Christ had achieved through his cross and resurrection, and a willingness to rethink everything in the light of this knowledge. Who was Christ, if he did something that only God can do? How could I make sense of Christ by taking this astonishing fact into account?

Third, I could hardly overlook the New Testament witness to Christ having been raised from the dead by God. While this event was clearly good news for believers, who will share that resurrection, I could see that it was also of importance to understanding the identity of Christ. For Paul, Jesus' resurrection tells us that he is the 'Son of God' (Romans 1:3–4). For Peter, it declares that he is the 'Lord and Messiah' (Acts 2:36).

Fourth, I found myself making a list of things that Jesus said and did which cast light on his identity. Mark's account of how Christ healed a paralytic (Mark 2:1–12) seemed especially illuminating to me. Christ declares to the paralytic that his sins are forgiven. This provokes outrage and astonishment on the part of the Jewish teachers of the law, who have been watching him closely. 'It is blasphemy! Who can forgive sins but God alone?' (Mark 2:7). I knew that they were right, and that I was confronted with a very important clue to the identity of Christ. One explanation was that he was a presumptuous fool; after all, there are plenty of these around. Another, however, seemed to me to be much more satisfying and challenging – that Christ indeed was justified in making this declaration. Christ had no right or authority whatsoever to speak those words *if he was just a human being*, like me. Yet Christ declares that he does indeed have such authority to forgive, and proceeds to heal the man (Mark 2:10–11).

Trying to get everything straight in my mind was not especially easy. Yet it forced me to wrestle with the question of how to do intellectual justice to Christ. He demanded to be understood to the limits of my ability. The conclusions that I reached were not startling. Others had reached them long before me, and they can be thought of as representing the settled common mind of Christians down the ages. But it was important for me to reach these conclusions for myself, rather than just passively accept what others had told me.

First, I concluded that Jesus was a genuine human being. He was someone who felt pain, who wept and who knew what it was like to be hungry and thirsty. Yet this insight, on its own, is clearly not enough to do justice to the biblical portrait of Jesus. It is not wrong, but inadequate. For the New Testament insists that Jesus was far more than a human being. God had to be brought into the picture somehow.

So my second conclusion was this. Without in any way denying the real humanity of Christ, I had to recognise him to be the Son of God. The New Testament applies words to him which are reserved for God, and attributes actions to him which are the privilege of God alone. Christ does what only God can do precisely because he is God and has the authority and ability to act in this way.

My two conclusions were the result of a long and passionate analysis of the total person of Christ – what he said and did, what was done to him and how people reacted to him. No other way of thinking about him seemed capable of doing justice to the biblical evidence.

I thus tried to know Christ with my mind, wanting to use my God-given reason to wrestle with the biblical witness to Christ in order to appreciate him fully. Knowing Christ as 'true God and true human' might seem like logical weakness. Yet it was clear to me that it was the only way of doing justice to the full significance of Jesus. If we were to give up one of the two insights noted above, we would end up with a much simpler yet ulti-mately inauthentic view of Christ. For example, it would be a lot easier to treat Christ simply as a human being, and to stop talking about him as God. Yet if Christ was only a human being, he could not redeem us. Only God can save. Nor could Christ reveal God to us. Only God can reveal himself. We would end up with a logically neat understanding of Jesus which distorts his identity and destroys the gospel.

The famous English novelist and amateur theologian Dorothy L. Sayers (1893–1957) stated the situation in words I found memorable and helpful: 'If Christ was only man, then he is entirely irrelevant to any thought about God; if he is only God, then he is entirely irrelevant to any experience of human life.' Using our minds to understand Christ more fully brings out how we need to affirm the 'two natures of Christ', and shows us what we lose if we deny it. But above all, it confirms the coherence of the Christian understanding of the identity of Jesus.

I learned much from this kind of reflection on the intellectual coherence and resilience of the Christian faith. Yet one of the hardest lessons anyone can learn is that our strengths have a deadly habit of becoming our weaknesses. Sometimes the things we do well can be a barrier to personal growth, because they prevent us from looking for other ways of doing things. My strength is my mind. I'm an academic sort of person, who naturally thinks in terms of understanding things – such as following an argument, or establishing the way in which ideas relate to each other. Yet this intellectual asset can easily become a spiritual liability. It led me to think of 'knowing Christ' purely in terms of knowing *about* Christ. I understood growth in faith to mean understanding more about the Christian faith, and especially about its central figure, Jesus Christ. Knowing Christ was nothing more and nothing less than gathering information *about* Christ. It was about an enhancement of my understanding. This way of thinking came naturally to me as an academic, and I assumed that it was the only and the best way. Yet, far from enriching my life of faith, it deadened it.

After a while, I began to realise that my faith had become stale. What had once been fresh and vigorous was dry and unrewarding. I responded in the only way I knew. I tried to learn more about Christ. I studied the geography of the Holy Land, so that I knew the exact location of all the places of significance to Christ's ministry. I memorised lots of names, dates and Bible verses. I certainly came away from this knowing more about my faith. But it remained detached, dry and dull. I had gained lots of information, but had lost something much deeper and more important – a sense of excitement about Christ. Something was wrong.

On reflection, it seemed to me that knowing Christ with our minds alone can lead us into two difficulties, each of which is a serious obstacle to knowing Christ in all his fulness and radiance.

First, we can fall into the intellectualist trap of thinking that 'knowing' is just 'knowing about' – the accumulation of facts – and thus fail to realise that knowing is a *relational* activity. When the King James Bible states that 'Adam knew Eve' (Genesis 4:1, 25) and subsequently bore him a child, a rather more intimate encounter is clearly envisaged. We must rediscover the hidden depths of the verb 'to know'. Christ does not want us to accumulate facts about him. He wants to embrace us and enfold us in his arms. He wants us to know him as Saviour, Lord and friend.

Second, we can commit the ultimate sin of intellectual arrogance and assume that, if we can't understand it, it can't be right. We therefore demand that the gospel should be expressed in terms that human reason can grasp. Unintentionally, the gospel thus comes to be imprisoned within the limits of human understanding. Our minds are no longer the servants of the gospel; they have become its master.

The results of this rationalist reduction of the Christian faith can easily be predicted. Christ is both human and divine? How can that be true? It involves a contradiction! Let's make things simpler: Jesus can be either divine, or human – but not both. We need to learn humility here, and be prepared to acknowledge the limitations placed on human understanding. 'If you can comprehend it, it's not God' (Augustine of Hippo). Can we really expect our fallen and finite human minds to be able to grasp the full radiance and glory of the risen Christ? Or the immensity of the God who created and redeemed us? It would be like asking a flea to appreciate the beauty of a Mozart symphony or the genius of Shakespeare's *Macbeth*. The limitations lie with the perceiver, not with what is to be perceived.

There is a story told about Augustine of Hippo (354–430), perhaps one of the greatest early Christian theologians. Augustine spent twenty years of his life writing a major treatise on the Christian understanding of God. According to this tale, Augustine was walking up and down the Mediterranean shoreline, deep in thought. How could he hope to express the immensity of God in human words? Were they up to the challenge? Engrossed in such thoughts, he suddenly noticed a small boy behaving strangely by the sea. The youngster would fill a container with water drawn from the sea, then pour it into a hole he had earlier dug in the sand. He then returned to the sea, refilled the container, and emptied its contents once more into the hole. And then the whole process was repeated, again and again.

Augustine watched this performance for a while, baffled by it. Eventually, he decided to intervene and ask the lad what he was doing. The boy duly informed Augustine that he was in the process of emptying the entire Mediterranean Sea into the small hole he had just dug in the sand. Augustine was astonished on hearing this explanation, and told the boy that he was completely wasting his time. He would never get the immensity of the ocean into such a small opening in the sand. Unperturbed by this piece of well-intended criticism, the boy responded vigorously: 'And you're wasting your time writing a book about God. You'll never get God into a book.'

Now there are just one or two reasons for suspecting that this story may not be entirely reliable! But the point made is of immense importance to our theme. The human mind is simply not big enough to comprehend God in all his glory. God can no more be embraced and enfolded by our minds than the Mediter-ranean Sea can be squeezed into a tiny hole on a beach. It is only by radically restricting God that we can accommodate him in this way – and this means *distorting* and *reducing* God. By demanding that our minds should be able to fully grasp every-thing, we risk reducing the gospel to a few common-sense platitudes.

Even though we may think of ourselves as wise and obedient Christians, we cannot entirely evade our tendency as finite and fallen human beings to construct out of the Gospels a Christ we can believe in. Without quite realising what we are doing, we reduce Christ to what we can manage to conceive, rather than allowing him to challenge us to open our minds and hearts to his immensity. We are predisposed to reduce Christ to what we can cope with, instead of allowing him to enlarge our apprehen-sion of his glory. We thus bring Christ down to our level, rather than allow him to raise us to his.

Part of the challenge we face in coming to know Christ is that of facing up to the limitations placed upon us by our human nature. A pagan emperor once visited the Jewish rabbi Joshua ben Hananiah, and asked to be allowed to see Joshua's god. The rabbi replied that this was totally impossible – an answer which naturally failed to satisfy the emperor. So the rabbi took the emperor outside, and asked him to stare at the midday summer sun. 'This is impossible!' replied the emperor. 'The human eye cannot cope with the brilliance of the sun!'

'If you cannot look at the sun, which God created,' replied the rabbi, 'how much less can you behold the glory of God himself.'

The point is clear, and of fundamental importance. If we are unable to perceive God's creation fully, how much less can we cope with God himself. There are limits placed upon our ability to discern God and cope with his radiance, and we must learn to identify and respect these.

Both the New Testament and Christian spiritual writers use the term 'mystery' to refer to the hidden depths of the Christian faith which stretch beyond the reach of reason. To speak of the 'mystery of Christ' is not to lapse into some kind of obscurantism or woolly way of thinking. It is simply to admit the limits placed upon our human reason, and the hold it can obtain on the living God. It is both realistic and humble, and reminds us that we shall only fully appreciate the radiance and majesty of the risen Christ when we enter into the halls of the New Jerusalem.

The Brazilian writer Leonardo Boff is aware of the importance of the concept of 'mystery' in relation to our growth in the Christian faith.

Seeing mystery in this perspective enables us to understand how it provokes reverence, the only possible attitude to what is supreme and final in our lives. Instead of strangling reason, it invites expansion of the mind and heart. It is not a mystery that leaves us dumb and terrified, but one that leaves us happy, singing and giving thanks. It is not a wall placed in front of us, but a doorway through which we go to the infinity of God. Mystery is like a cliff: we may not be able to scale it, but we can stand at the foot of it, touch it, praise its beauty.[2]

What we can know about Christ is good and trustworthy. It is not, however, a *full* disclosure of Christ. For that, we shall have to wait until we have left our frail and fallen human natures behind, and have been raised in glory. As Paul put this point: 'now we see in a mirror, dimly, but then we will see face to face' (1 Corinthians 13:12).

We have many unanswered questions concerning Christ which we shall never be able to answer in this life. We must rejoice at what we do know, and eagerly anticipate what we do not yet know in all its fulness. Yet, as Paul reassures us, we shall one day see Christ face to face, and know him as he knows us (1 Corinthians 13:12). Perhaps then we shall have answers to those perplexing questions that once troubled us. Yet maybe being in the presence of our Saviour will make them seem hardly worth asking.

2

Knowing Christ in our imaginations

The neuropsychologists tell us that the two sides of the human brain respond in significantly different ways to the stimuli which they receive. The left hemisphere is especially associated with logical analysis and rational judgements. The right hemisphere, however, has a special affinity with visual imagery and emotionally laden words. Some people have dominant left hemispheres, others dominant right hemispheres. This has a significant impact on how we respond to words we read, or hear read to us. Words which demand rational analysis can be thought of as activating the left hemisphere, while those which generate imagery or emotions activate the right. This has two important implications for the way in which we read and benefit from Scripture.

First, it means that we should expect to mingle logical analysis and image-based meditation in our reflections on Scripture. Either on its own is inadequate to Scripture itself, as a careful study of its uses of words makes clear; it is also inadequate in terms of the way we are as thinking human beings. Our minds, hearts and imaginations must be brought together as we seek to gain the most from our engagement with Scripture.

Second, it means that different individuals will find that they are impacted in significantly different ways by the text of

Scripture. Some will find themselves excited by the challenge of the logical analysis of the ideas of Scripture, traditionally associated with the discipline of systematic theology. Others will find themselves drawn to the visual imagery and its emotional impact, and may want to try and express this in terms of art or poetry. It must be stressed that both are legitimate. The systematic theologian who despises the poet or artist has probably failed to appreciate the immense richness of the gospel, and has fallen into the most subtle yet deadly of traps – thinking that the way they see things is the way things really are.

As you will have gathered, I am a very verbal person, used to thinking in words. While there is nothing wrong with this, it does have an important implication for my spirituality. It means that I tend to focus on ideas. Now let me make it clear once more that ideas matter profoundly to the Christian faith. We do not just believe *in* Christ; we believe certain quite definite things *about* Christ. Understanding these properly is an essential element of our Christian discipleship. We do not simply trust Christ; we believe that he is totally worthy of such trust. Yet the heart of Christianity is a person, not an idea. Christ himself *is* the truth; he does not simply *show* or *tell* us the truth (John 14:6). Christ embodies the message which he proclaims and which is proclaimed in his name.

I first became aware of the limitations of a very verbal approach to my faith through reading a late medieval writer. I had been working on Ludolf of Saxony (c. 1300–78) as part of my preparation for a course I was teaching at Oxford. We know little about him, except that he was deeply concerned to help his readers gain a deeper apprehension of Christ as Lord and Saviour. For Ludolf, it was not enough for readers to simply *understand* what was going on in a story from the Gospels. To get the most out of any Gospel passage, the reader had to enter into it, allowing its vivid and realistic account of events to impact powerfully on their imaginations. I found myself being challenged and greatly assisted by Ludolf's book *The Life of Christ*, in which he sets out the approach he uses to get the most out of reading the Gospel accounts of the life of Jesus:

> Go with the Wise Men to Bethlehem and adore the little king. Help his parents carry the child and present him in the Temple. Alongside the apostles, accompany the Good Shepherd as he performs his miracles. With his blessed mother and St John, be there at his death, to have compassion on him and to grieve with him. Touch his body with a kind of devout curiosity, handling one by one the wounds of your Saviour who has died for you. With Mary Magdalene seek the risen Christ until you are found worthy to find him. Look with wonder at his ascent into heaven as though you were standing among his disciples on the Mount of Olives.[3]

As someone who naturally thinks in terms of ideas, I was anxious – even suspicious – of any appeal to the 'imagination'. I saw an uncomfortably close connection between the words 'imaginary' and 'imagination'. Surely an appeal to the imagination implied a lack of respect for the historical reliability of the Gospels? These were fair concerns.

Yet there need be no tension here. I regard it as a historical fact that Christ died upon a cross. This is a truth which is of supreme importance to the Christian faith, and to my personal devotion. Yet I do not call the historical factuality of this event into question by trying to imagine what it was like. In any case, historical events demand to be visualised. We know history properly when we allow our imaginations to play out its chapters in the theatre of our minds, and see things happening as if we were present to witness them for ourselves. By bringing my biblically informed imagination to bear on the event of Calvary, I was able to appreciate the poignancy, passion and pain of Christ's saving death far more powerfully and authentically than by reading the pages of some dense and dusty work of theology.

The Bible is richly studded with imagery, and it is essential to our spiritual growth that we reflect on that imagery. We do indeed find propositional statements concerning God – for example, St John's wonderful affirmation that 'God is love'. Yet revelation often takes the form of images and metaphors – for example, when God is declared to be a rock, a shepherd or a king. The book of Revelation is perhaps the most visual work within Scripture, parading before us a plethora of highly evocative images which demand to be mulled over.

Propositions limit meaning; images evoke wonder while they challenge us to unlock their meanings. As I began to reflect on how best to release the revelational potential of biblical images, I realised that I was being challenged to engage the biblical text at a far deeper level than before. Instead of woodenly agreeing with the Psalmist that 'the Lord is my shepherd', I was being invited to generate a mental image of a shepherd in action, and *see* him guiding his sheep, leading them to green pastures and protecting them from predators. I was being encouraged to visualise God in this way, as a means of going beyond a purely verbal way of thinking about God. The words of Scripture impact upon our imaginations as we allow them to be reconstituted as visual realities; in this way they both illuminate our faith and enable us to grasp at least something of the wonder they are meant to evoke.

While reflecting on this point, I came across Gerard of Zutphen (1367–1400), who stressed the importance of meditating on Scripture and allowing what I read to stimulate my imagination and reflection. I found these words immensely helpful.

Meditation is the process in which you diligently turn over in your heart whatever you have read or heard, earnestly reflecting upon it and thus enkindling your affections in some particular manner, or enlightening your understanding.[4]

Just as I had been suspicious of the word 'imagination', I also had anxieties about the word 'meditation'. I had been encouraged to think that this was the sort of thing that Buddhists emphasised, and that it was therefore totally off-limits for Christians. Yet this, I was to discover, was quite misguided. Didn't the Psalmist declare his intention to 'meditate on all your work, and muse on your mighty deeds' (Psalm 77:12)? Certain Buddhist schools of meditation do indeed encourage people to empty their minds of all distracting thoughts and focus their attention on whatever comes to mind. For the Christian, however, meditation is about clearing one's mind of all distractions, in order that it may focus on a biblical image – such as God as a shepherd – or a biblical passage. The biblically informed believing imagination can then begin to bring these images to life and allow a new quality of engagement with the biblical revelation.

In the case of reading Gospel passages, I began to think of myself as being there, witnessing what is said and done. I began to read the Gospel narratives with new excitement. The mental effort which I had to make to project myself into the biblical world meant that I appreciated what I found all the more. Ludolf forced me to stand beside various key actors in the biblical narrative, and join them as the drama of human redemption unfolded in front of their eyes – and mine.

My life of prayer was immeasurably enriched by this procedure. No longer was I simply registering ideas as I read. I was reliving the historical events on which my faith was grounded. Instead of skimming along the surface of biblical narratives, I was beginning to become part of them, being challenged and encouraged by them. Meditating on the biblical text led to my entering into the world which it described. Ludolf of Saxony again provided me with some wise advice when reflecting on such biblical passages.

If you want to draw fruit from these, you must offer yourself as present to what was said and done through our Lord Jesus

Christ with the whole affective power of your mind, with loving care, with lingering delight, thus laying aside all other worries and care.

Meditation was about using 'the whole affective power of your mind, with loving care, with lingering delight' and allowing my imagination to be stimulated and guided by what I found in Scripture. Before I had looked *at* biblical images; now I began to look *through* them, as they became windows of perception. Scripture teaches us that we have been made in the image of God (Genesis 1:27). Is it therefore surprising that Scripture itself uses images so extensively and powerfully, or that humanity is able to gain so much from prayerful reflection upon them? The rich panoply of biblical imagery guides, stimulates and nourishes us in our journey of faith. It helps us to picture the reality in which we now find ourselves, and to look forward to the greater reality in which we shall one day take our rest.

Countless Christian writers have realised the importance of this point, and done something about it. A good example is provided by the famous hymn by Isaac Watts (1674–1748), 'When I survey the wondrous cross'. As Watts uses his imagination to build up a mental picture of the crucifixion, he is able to meditate on the pain and shame of the dying Christ, and thus realises the shallowness of his response to his Saviour.

> When I survey the wondrous Cross
> On which the Prince of Glory died,
> My richest gain I count but loss,
> And pour contempt on all my pride.
>
> Forbid it, Lord, that I should boast
> Save in the Cross of Christ my Lord.
> All the vain things that charm me most,
> I sacrifice them to his blood.

See from his head, his hands, his feet
Sorrow and love flow mingled down;
Did e'er such love and sorrow meet?
Or thorns compose so rich a crown?

His dying crimson, like a robe,
Spreads o'er his body on the tree;
Then I am dead to all the globe,
And all the globe is dead to me.

Were the whole realm of nature mine,
That were an offering far too small;
Love so amazing, so divine,
Demands my soul, my life, my all.[5]

Notice how Watts uses his imagination, especially in the third and fourth verses, to build up a verbal picture of the cross, focusing attention on the pain experienced by the dying Christ. Watts makes the point that there is nothing that can equal in magnitude the offering made by Christ. But we can at least try, by offering ourselves to Christ in order that his love might be made known to all. It is an important point to make – but notice how he makes it. He provides a series of word-prompts, which trigger the imagination into evoking that most powerful and pathetic image of a bruised, bleeding and dying Saviour. By meditating on that mental image, we can recapture something of the poignancy of the first Good Friday.

For this is the point: we were not there at Calvary to see Christ die. We were not privileged to witness Christ placed upon the cross and raised up on high for us. We were not able to see the wounds which healed us, or hear the last words from the cross – words which spoke of suffering and death for our Saviour, but life and hope for us. Yet we want to be able to appreciate the costliness of that redemption, in order to honour and adore him. Our imaginations offer a window into that Calvary scene, unlocking its potential to move us to tears of sadness and joy, affecting both our mind and heart.

So how is Christ to be known in our hearts?

3

Knowing Christ in our hearts

Paul prayed that Christ might dwell within the hearts of his readers (Ephesians 3:17). To know Christ is to know his presence in our hearts. I vividly remember a conversation some years ago with Donald Coggan, a former archbishop of Canterbury. We were discussing some of the challenges to theological education, and had ended by sharing our concerns over people who left theological education knowing a lot more about God but seemingly loving God rather less than when they came in. Coggan turned to me sadly and remarked: 'The journey from head to heart is one of the longest and most difficult that we know.' I have often reflected on that comment, which I suspect reflects his lifelong interest in theological education and the considerable frustrations it generated – not to mention his experiences of burnt-out clergy, who seemed to have exhausted their often slender resources of spiritual energy and ended up becoming a burden instead of a gift to the people of God.

A head-knowledge of God may well be better than no knowledge of God at all. But it leaves a lot to be desired. Why? Let me answer this question by recalling a famous episode from English church history. In May 1738, John Wesley (1703–91) attended a meeting in Aldersgate Street, London. Wesley already knew all about the Christian faith and had a good understanding of the basics of Christian doctrine. He knew about Christ. Yet, as events made clear, he did not really know him. At this meeting, Wesley listened to a speaker reading from one of Martin Luther's works. As he did so, he felt his heart to be 'strangely warmed'. It was as if what he knew in his mind had been applied to his heart. Here is Wesley's journal entry for that day:

> In the evening I went very unwillingly to a society in Aldersgate Street, where someone was reading Luther's preface to the Epistle to the Romans. About a quarter before nine, while he was describing the change which God works in the heart through faith in Christ, I felt my heart strangely warmed. I felt I did trust in Christ, Christ alone, for salvation; and an assurance was given me that he had taken away my sins, even mine, and saved me from the law of sin and death.[6]

Wesley's remarks bring home to us how important it is to know Christ in our hearts, not simply in our minds. It is not enough to know Christ by description; we must know him within the intimacy of a relationship. It is perfectly possible to know about Christ without having encountered him as a living and life-changing reality. *We can easily assent to the truth of the gospel, yet find something else more attractive and meaningful.* Our mind may assent to the truth of Christ, but our hearts find their consolation through someone or something else. Our hearts must recognise Christ as the fulfilment of all their secret desires and longings before we can truly know him.

I can know about a person – for example, the President of the United States. Yet this implies no commitment or interest on that person's part for me. It is a one-way street. A relationship implies privilege – the willingness of the other person to become interested in me; to want to spend time with me; to esteem me as worth knowing. While mulling over such points in my mind, I came across some words from a writer who had influenced

John Wesley to no small extent. Count Nicolas von Zinzendorf (1700–60) argued that it was relational, not intellectual, knowledge which was the more satisfying and enduring. Here are the words I found so challenging:

> An understanding which arises out of concepts changes with age, education, and other circumstances. An understanding arrived at through experience is not subject to these changes; such understanding becomes better with time and circumstances.

The point that Zinzendorf was making was simple, but so important. We can get bored with ideas. What was once new becomes stale through familiarity. Yet a relationship – something which enters into and changes our lives – is totally different. It is like getting to know and rely upon someone who becomes a trustworthy friend, in whose company we luxuriate. Ideas lose their freshness, but friends remain by our sides.

To know Christ is a wonderful thing. Yet it is a still more wonderful matter that Christ knows us. *We are known by him*. The one who died for us on Calvary knows each of us by name. The purpose of his journey into the far country was to bring us home, rejoicing. He is our shepherd, whose care for us never falters. This is one of the most wonderful truths that the Christian faith proclaims. The God who created the heavens and earth stooped down to enter human history in Christ, to suffer rejection and pain, and finally to die. Why? *For us*. For Luther, these two words ought to be written in golden letters on the hearts of every Christian believer. They speak to us of a Saviour who *wants* to be known, who longs to grant us the privilege of friendship with him.

I have become so used to the idea of being close to Christ that I often lose sight of the immense privilege of this relationship. Familiarity, we are told, breeds contempt. In my case it gave rise to a certain complacency. I needed to be reminded of just how privileged we are to have such a relationship with Christ. It was while reading Ignatius Loyola's *Spiritual Exercises* for the first time that I came across a very helpful approach, which allowed me to rediscover the privilege of knowing and being known by Christ.

In the *Spiritual Exercises*, Loyola (1491–1556) suggests that one of the best ways of appreciating the immense relational privilege Christ confers upon us is to see ourselves against a cosmic background. When we realise how small, insignificant and sinful we are, we cannot help but be overwhelmed by the amazing fact that Christ wants to know us. Loyola suggests we think along five lines of comparison, as follows:

> First, I shall reflect upon how much I am in comparison to all other human beings;
> Second, what other human beings are in comparison to all the angels and saints of paradise;
> Third, what all creation is in comparison to God.
> So if I think of myself alone, what can I be?
> Fourth, to see all my bodily corruption and foulness;
> Fifth, to look at myself as a sore and ulcer, from which so many sins, iniquities and poisons have sprung.[7]

As I worked through these five points, I began to understand how insignificant I was. You may find it helpful to work through them as well, perhaps using my own reflections as a basis for your thinking.

First, Loyola asks us to see our own individual existence against the backdrop of every other human being living on this planet. What am I in comparison with these billions of people? How am I going to get noticed? Why should anyone care especially for me, when there are countless others competing for attention in this world?

Second, each of these human beings is vastly inferior to those who now live in paradise – the saints, who have 'fought the good fight' and finally entered into the presence of God. They are far more important than I am. So why should Christ want anything much to do with me?

Third, we need to see ourselves against the vast backdrop of the cosmos – against the immense distances of space. Perhaps it is easier for us to do this today than it was in the sixteenth century. We have become increasingly aware that the earth is simply one planet circling an unimportant star in an unimportant galaxy consisting of billions of stars. And countless other, greater galaxies lie scattered throughout the silent void of the universe. And God is still greater than this creation!

Putting these three thoughts together, Loyola asks us to reflect on what significance each of us, on our own, could possibly have. Each of us represents less than one billionth of the present living human population of Planet Earth, which is an infinitesimally small speck of dust in comparison with the rest of the universe . . . These thoughts certainly put things in perspective.

But Loyola has only just begun to explore our insignificance. Having demonstrated that each of us represents a diminutive fragment of God's complete creation, he now goes on to make two additional points. And what do these tell us? Not only are we insignificant, we are sinful, and potentially a source of corruption within God's good creation. It is helpful to follow through the lines of reflection set out in these fourth and fifth points.

Fourth, Ignatius makes the telling point that we are sinful and must appreciate that this is the case. We may like to think of ourselves as upright and spiritually healthy, but the reality is rather different. We are wounded and corrupted. It is bad enough to be insignificant and good; Loyola gently suggests that we will just have to come to terms with the fact that we are insignificant and sinful.

Fifth, we have to take this depressing insight a stage further and realise that we are potentially the source of corruption and evil in others.

It is easy to reject this humiliating assault on our self-worth as some kind of spiritual guilt trip. Yet this will not do. The insights that Loyola asks us to develop are painfully true. If we are to know Christ, we will have to face up to the fact that there is nothing about us that merits such a privileged relationship.

The more we realise our personal unworthiness, the more we appreciate the privilege of knowing Christ – personally.

Loyola helped me understand the privilege of knowing Christ by allowing me to grasp the painful nettle of personal unworthiness and sin, while realising that Christ loved me and wanted to know me – as he wanted to be known by me.

I found my appreciation of the privilege of knowing Christ in this way further enhanced by reading some of the poems of George Herbert (1593–1633). Herbert had a particular genius for being able to unpack the spiritual implications of Christian theology and use powerful imagery as a means of allowing his readers to gain insights which they had hitherto overlooked. His collection of religious poems, *The Temple*, was published shortly after his death in 1633. The closing poem of the collection – entitled 'Love' – can be seen as an extended musing on how it can be that Christ can possibly love a sinner. Throughout the poem, Christ is referred to as 'Love'. You will find it helpful to read the poem before I share the insights that I gained from engaging with it.

Love bade me welcome, yet my soul drew back,
    Guilty of dust and sin.
But quick-ey'd Love, observing me grow slack
    From my first entrance in,
Drew nearer to me, sweetly questioning
    If I lack'd anything.

'A guest,' I answer'd, 'worthy to be here';
    Love said, 'You shall be he.'
'I, the unkind, the ungrateful? ah my dear,

    I cannot look on thee.'
  Love took my hand and smiling did reply,
    'Who made the eyes but I?'

    'Truth, Lord, but I have marr'd them; let my shame
      Go where it doth deserve.'
    'And know you not,' says Love, 'who bore the blame?'
      'My dear, then I will serve.'
    'You must sit down,' says Love, 'and taste my meat.'
      So I did sit and eat.[8]

The first verse of the poem invites us to imagine ourselves as approaching Christ, attracted to him yet at the same time aware of our own weakness and failings. Why should such a wonderful, pure and righteous Saviour want anything to do with someone who was 'guilty of dust and sin'? Why should the creator stoop down to greet the creature, or the Saviour to embrace the sinner? Yet Herbert asks us to imagine Christ noticing our hesitation and moving swiftly to greet and reassure us.

    Is there anything that we would like? When I first read these lines, I was reminded of some of the scenes from the *Arabian Nights*, in which a genie appears, offering to grant three wishes. What is your heart's desire? Herbert's answer to Love's question would have been my answer: he wanted to be worthy to be Love's guest. Yet the request seemed beyond his reach. How could someone so insignificant and guilty ever be welcomed into the presence of the Son of God? Herbert sets out clearly why he believes that this is impossible. He is so unworthy that he should not even be allowed to gaze upon Christ from a distance, let alone be welcomed into his presence. Yet Love reassures him once more – this time, through *taking him by the hand*. Just as Christ was willing to touch and hold sinners and lepers, so he takes hold of us. Why? As the poem progresses, we learn his reason for doing so. Christ 'bore the blame' for our sin, so that it need no longer be a barrier between sinner and Saviour. Through taking us by the hand, Christ leads us to sit down at table with him. A privilege which we would not dare to claim is presented to us. We are led by our Lord and Saviour to sit at table with him.

In the third verse, we find a deeply moving reflection on the sense of unworthiness felt by Herbert. Even though he knows that Christ loves him and has willingly borne his guilt, he believes that he has been welcomed into Christ's presence as a servant — as one who is to wait on Christ. The poem ends with an exquisite portrayal of the hesitant believer being welcomed as an honoured guest, not as an attendant servant. As I read the poem over and over again, I found myself being deeply moved by its vivid and gentle depiction of a gracious Saviour welcoming to his side those who knew that they were totally unworthy of his company. Yet the Lord promises to be at our side for ever in this life, until we finally sit down at table with him in the New Jerusalem. We can anticipate this wonderful reunion with Christ in the future, just as we can look back on his cross and resurrection as secure grounds for this hope.

Such thoughts lead us on to consider the role of memory in knowing Christ.

4

Knowing Christ in our memories

'Remember!' This theme resonates throughout the history of the people of God. They are to remember who they are. They are to remember how they came into being. And they are to remember the words and deeds of the creator and Saviour God who has called them, and remains their comforter and guide to this day.

One of the greatest stories that has ever been told concerns how the people of Israel were delivered from their harsh bondage in Egypt and led through the wilderness into the Promised Land of Canaan. It was a formative era for Israel, during which she had to learn the privileges and responsibilities of being the people of God. During this period, the crystallisation of Israel's understanding of the nature and character of her God began to set in. Lessons were learned that should never be forgotten.

Yet forgotten they were. As Israel settled down in the Promised Land, she began to take everything for granted. The humble and simple tents of the period of wandering were discarded, to be replaced with fine stone houses richly panelled with wood. Straddling some of the most strategic trade routes of the ancient world, Israel grew rich. As she became prosperous, she became complacent and indifferent to her past heritage and present responsibilities. The God who had led her from captivity to prosperity was marginalised.

It is no wonder that the great prophets of the Old Testament were appalled at Israel's behaviour. Her identity and mission as the people of God would be compromised unless she were to reclaim and reappropriate her privileged legacy as the chosen people. A leading theme of their call to renewal and repentance was therefore that of *recollection* – meaning both 'remembering' and 'picking up again'. So how was this remembering to be encouraged? And what would be gained by it?

First, it reminded Israel of the great events in history that brought her into being. The festival of Passover was to be a permanent memorial of the mighty acts of God, which led to Israel being liberated from bondage in Egypt: 'Remember this day on which you came out of Egypt, out of the house of slavery, because the LORD brought you out from there by strength of hand' (Exodus 13:3). After Israel settled in the Promised Land, she was to continue reminding herself that her presence in that land was a divine gift and privilege.

Second, it confronted Israel with the faithfulness and power of her God. If Israel needed any reminder of that faithfulness and might, all she need do was meditate on the past, recalling all that God had done in history. Psalm 136 is perhaps the greatest of these calls to recollection, reminding Israel of all that God had done, in the creation of the world and the calling and redemption of his people Israel.

Psalm 136:3–22

O give thanks to the Lord of lords, for his steadfast love
　　endures for ever;
who alone does great wonders, for his steadfast love endures
　　for ever;
who by understanding made the heavens, for his steadfast
　　love endures for ever;
who spread out the earth on the waters, for his steadfast
　　love endures for ever;
who made the great lights, for his steadfast love endures for
　　ever;
the sun to rule over the day, for his steadfast love endures
　　for ever;
the moon and stars to rule over the night, for his steadfast
　　love endures for ever;
who struck Egypt through their firstborn, for his steadfast
　　love endures for ever;
and brought Israel out from among them, for his steadfast
　　love endures for ever;
with a strong hand and an outstretched arm, for his steadfast
　　love endures for ever;
who divided the Red Sea in two, for his steadfast love
　　endures for ever;
and made Israel pass through the midst of it, for his steadfast
　　love endures for ever;
but overthrew Pharaoh and his army in the Red Sea, for
　　his steadfast love endures for ever;
who led his people through the wilderness, for his steadfast
　　love endures for ever;
who struck down great kings, for his steadfast love endures
　　for ever;

and killed famous kings, for his steadfast love endures for
ever;
Sihon, king of the Amorites, for his steadfast love endures
for ever;
and Og, king of Bashan, for his steadfast love endures for
ever;
and gave their land as a heritage, for his steadfast love
endures for ever;
a heritage to his servant Israel, for his steadfast love endures
for ever.

There are two things which this Psalm achieves through its
constant reiteration of the general principle of the enduring
love of God and the specific illustrations which it provides of
this divine graciousness.

First, it lists the actions of God in the past which demonstrate
his love for Israel and commitment to her. The Psalm offers a
survey of the mighty acts of God in the creation of the world
and the calling and redemption of Israel. Each of these acts in
itself merits detailed study and reflection; taken together, they
fuse to provide a panorama of God's actions which demonstrates
his total commitment to the well-being of his people. By
remembering and meditating on these actions, we can be
reassured of the constancy of God's graciousness and goodness.

Second, the Psalm makes the critically important point that
God's love is demonstrated in God's actions. To speak of the love
of God is to speak of the deeds of God which confirm and
embody that love. We find the same point made in the New
Testament, especially in the first letter of John. For John, 'God is
love'. Yet this love is corroborated in action – supremely, the
sending of God's Son into the world to win our salvation.

God's love was revealed among us in this way: God sent his only Son into the world so that we might live through him. In this is love, not that we loved God, but that he loved us and sent his Son to be the atoning sacrifice for our sins.

(1 John 4:9–10)

God's character is rendered in his actions; remembering and reflecting on God's past actions thus enables us to appreciate his past faithfulness, and trust in that faithfulness in the future. The God to whom both Old and New Testaments bear witness is the same God with whom we have to deal today. *Remembering what God has done allows us to anticipate what God will do.*

So what bearing do these reflections have on our theme of knowing Christ? The answer is two-fold. First, we can remember what Christ has done for us in history, supremely in his death upon the cross for us. It is of no small importance here to appreciate that Christ lived, acted, spoke, was put to death and rose again as a historical figure. To remember Jesus is thus to gain a renewed and deepened understanding of who he is and what he achieved.

The importance of this point is undergirded by the explicit command of Christ to remember him through the breaking of bread.

For I received from the Lord what I also handed on to you, that the Lord Jesus on the night when he was betrayed took a loaf of bread, and when he had given thanks, he broke it and said, 'This is my body that is for you. Do this in remembrance of me.' In the same way he took the cup also, after supper, saying, 'This cup is the new covenant in my blood. Do this, as often as you drink it, in remembrance of me.' For as often as you eat this bread and drink the cup, you proclaim the Lord's death until he comes.

(1 Corinthians 11:23–6)

The bread and wine thus become the triggers for our memory of what Christ achieved for us on the cross, in much the same way as the Passover ceremony reminded Jews of the exodus from Egypt. The Old Testament prophets had to remind Israel of all that God had done for her during her numerous moments of forgetfulness or denial. We must do the same, by constantly calling to mind all that Christ suffered and achieved for us.

Second, we can remember all that Christ has already done for us – the blessings which he has brought us. Remembering what Christ has already done in our lives is a way of anticipating what he might do in the future. It is also an important way of challenging us about the quality of our relationship with Christ. Have we lost something? If so, what can be done to recover it? Has our passion for Christ waned? If so, what can we do to renew that ardour? The church at Laodicea became lukewarm towards Christ, causing a spurned and neglected Saviour and Lord to knock at their door, asking to become part of their lives once more (Revelation 3:20). Do we need to hear him knocking for readmission to our lives?

We can see this kind of spiritual strategy being developed in Psalm 42. This is a Psalm of lament for a loss of confidence in God, for a weakening of faith. Yet it mingles sorrow over this loss with anticipation of renewal and recovery. The Psalmist's soul is 'cast down' because he feels far from God, longing for his renewed presence. Yet he looks *backwards* before looking *forward*. He recalls the moments of spiritual intimacy and confidence in the past, and allows these to encourage him for the future.

These things I remember as I pour out my soul: how I went with the throng, and led them in procession to the house of God, with glad shouts and songs of thanksgiving, a multitude keeping festival. Why are you cast down, O my soul, and why are you disquieted within me? Hope in God; for I shall again praise him, my help and my God.

(Psalm 42:4–6)

Recalling the past is a stimulus to recovering the state of affairs which has now been lost.

This same strategy can be used in encouraging spiritual intimacy with Christ. Recalling how we have known Christ is an important stimulus to recovering past intimacy, excitement and joy – things which can easily become eroded in the life of faith. Contrasting a present lukewarmness towards Christ with a past passion for him allows two critical insights.

1   *It tells us that something is wrong.* Sin deceives us, and we are often willing accomplices to this deception. We like to think that all is well in our spiritual lives, and are reluctant to face up to the threat posed by an erosion of faith or commitment. Yet becoming aware that there is a problem is essential to working for improvement. The Lord gently chided Israel with memories of their moments of intimacy in the period of wandering in the wilderness (Hosea 11:1–4). Those past moments were lost. Hosea portrays the Lord as longing for them to be recalled, and for his relationship with his people to be renewed. We must be prepared to hear such criticisms of our present spiritual state; our memories can provide precisely such a much-needed challenge. Memory can challenge complacency.

2   *It offers us hope for renewal.* Wherever Scripture offers a criticism of the spiritual state of individuals or communities, it also offers the hope of change and recovery. Hosea challenged his wayward people to recommit themselves to the Lord, and receive healing and forgiveness as a result: 'I will heal their disloyalty, I will love them freely, for my anger has turned from them. I will be like the dew to Israel; he shall blossom like the lily' (Hosea 14:4–5). We

find the same graciousness in Christ's challenge to the
church at Laodicea, which had become lukewarm towards
him. 'Listen! I am standing at the door, knocking. If
you hear my voice and open the door, I will come in to
you and eat with you, and you with me' (Revelation 3:20).

Yet memory is linked with anticipation. We look backwards to
remind ourselves of all that Christ has done for us, and find
ourselves reassured of his trustworthiness. This gives us renewed
confidence that he will indeed fulfil the great promises which
he has made to us for the future – such as raising us to eternal
life. As Paul pointed out, all of God's promises find their 'Yes!' in
Christ (2 Corinthians 1:20). Christ is the ground and guarantor
of the promises of God. How do we know that we can trust
these promises? In one sense, by remembering all that Christ has
done.

It is here that we need to introduce the theme of the fulfilment
of Old Testament prophecy. What the prophets anticipated, Christ
fulfilled. Limits on space make it impossible to do more than
sketch some of the ways in which the New Testament highlights
how Old Testament hopes were fulfilled in Christ. In his account
of the birth of Christ, Matthew draws his readers' attention to
the remarkable parallels between the circumstances of that birth
and the prophecies of the Old Testament, drawing our attention
to this point no fewer than five times in his first two chapters
(Matthew 1:22–3; 2:5–7; 2:15; 2:17–18; 2:23). The passion
narratives of the Gospels bring out subtly the remarkable parallels between the 'Righteous Sufferer' of Psalm 22 and the
suffering and dying Christ. Christ's tragic words of despair 'My
God, my God, why have you forsaken me?' (Matthew 27:46)
point to this mysterious Psalm, and particularly to its description
of the Righteous Sufferer. This figure is mocked by those who
watch him die (Psalm 22:6–8), as is Christ (Matthew 27.39–44).
He has his hands and feet pierced (Psalm 22:16), as would those
who were crucified. He sees his tormentors casting lots for his

clothes (Psalm 22:18), as does Christ (Matthew 27:35).

The crucifixion is also anticipated in the remarkable account of the 'Suffering Servant' of Isaiah 53, as Luke notes explicitly in his account of the passion of Christ (Luke 22:37). This famous Old Testament prophecy speaks of a Suffering Servant of God, who was 'wounded for our transgressions, crushed for our iniquities' (Isaiah 53:5). Perhaps the most significant part of this prophecy relates to the fact that the Servant is 'numbered with the transgressors' (Isaiah 53:12), which is clearly understood by the Gospel writers to be paralleled in two manners. First, Christ died by crucifixion, which was a mode of death then reserved for criminals. Christ was thus identified with sinners by the manner of his death. Second, Christ was not crucified alone, but alongside two criminals (Matthew 27:38). In his suffering and death – as in his ministry – he was found with sinners. In both ways, Christ's death was realised to parallel that of an important Old Testament figure. Other parallels with this account may be seen in the Gospels, although they are not pointed out by the Gospel writers. Thus Luke notes that Jesus prayed for his executioners (Luke 23:34), paralleling the actions of the Suffering Servant (Isaiah 53:12). It seems clear that the first Christians could not help but notice the obvious parallels between the life and death of Jesus and certain significant prophecies of the Old Testament, and take a certain degree of delight in pointing them out to their readers, or allowing them to discover them for themselves.

What the Old Testament writers anticipated, Christ delivered. And by remembering that he fulfilled the great hopes and expectations of the Old Testament, we can urge ourselves on to new levels of trust and confidence in this most trustworthy God. To know Christ in our memories thus reinforces our present trust in God, and our future anticipation of finally reigning with him in heaven, where he has gone to prepare a place for us.

PART 2

When Christ is to be known

'I am with you always, to the end of the age' (Matthew 28:20). Having commissioned his disciples to bring the gospel to the ends of the earth, Christ adds his personal promise to this most powerful of charges. He will be with us to the end of time. He will be there for us, no matter what that uncertain future may hold. Abraham left everything and set off from his home town to the distant and unknown land of Canaan. He knew that the Lord who had called him would be with him as he journeyed, and that this most gracious and caring God had a purpose in mind in calling him to do this (Genesis 12:1–5).

So it is with us. Christ has called us to leave the cares of the world behind, and seek the hidden riches of the kingdom of God. Yet perhaps the greatest of all those riches is the promise of his glorious presence, to illuminate our lives and warm our cold hearts. He is there always, whether we know that in our experience or not. And in contemplating Christ, we find our heart's desire. This point was made powerfully by Charles Haddon Spurgeon (1834–92): 'There is, in contemplating Christ, a balm for every wound.' Spurgeon here rightly located the source of all spiritual nourishment, comfort and stimulus in the contemplation of Christ. Indeed, his preaching ministry may be said to represent an extended exploration of exactly such a contemplation of Christ.

There may be times when the clouds of anxiety, sadness, distraction and fear come between us and the radiance of Christ our sun, dulling his light and overshadowing the verdant pastures of our walk with him. Yet he is always there. Even when we forget about him, we are constantly in his thoughts. There is no moment when his kindly gaze leaves us, or when we walk alone and unloved. We are constantly enfolded in his care, as our Saviour and Lord, shielded from the power of our enemies.

Yet there are moments when Christ draws especially close to us, and allows the radiance of his presence to console us. Although we can be assured that Christ is with us at all times and in all places, it is often when we walk through the 'valley of the shadow of death' that we need and value his presence most greatly. It is then that we take the greatest comfort from the warmth of his healing presence. And it is then that our Lord draws close to us, taking us by the hand and leading us onwards and upwards. Whatever we have to face, we face with him, and not on our own or in our own strength.

In this section, our particular concern is with those moments and situations in which we need to know Christ with special intimacy, or in which he draws close to us in our weakness. When we are at our weakest, our eyes turn once more to Christ as the true source of our strength. When other voices are silent, we are most willing to hear Christ's words of comfort and challenge. When others pass us by, we turn again to rediscover the tender embrace of our Lord. It is in such moments of vulnerability that Christ draws near, seeking to renew and redirect us. Such moments may be rare for some, common for others. They are always precious, in that they help us refocus both thoughts and lives.

With this point in mind, we may turn to consider how loneliness can be a window of opportunity for knowing Christ more fully.

5

Knowing Christ in loneliness

The Christian life is not easy, and there are moments when we feel lost and lonely. At times we are like Elijah, feeling that we are just about the only people on the face of the earth who care for the Lord. Both Old and New Testaments teach us to think of ourselves as 'sojourners' or 'wayfarers' – people who are passing through this world, but whose true destiny and home lies somewhere else. We do not belong here. We are like the Roman citizens in Philippi, who served their empire in this foreign city but who longed to return home to where they really belonged. We are 'citizens of heaven', not citizens of this world. We live in this world as ones who know that our true homeland is ahead of us.

The Old Testament offers us an image which can help us make sense of our time in this world. The image is the great theme of the exodus from Egypt, followed by the wandering in the wilderness and eventually the triumphant entry into the Promised Land. Israel was led out of captivity in Egypt by a great act of divine deliverance; many Christians can recall a moment in their lives in which they were also liberated from the bondage and despair of sin and began a new way of life as Christians. Yet that wonderful deliverance did not lead directly into the Promised Land. There was a period of wandering through the wilderness, in which Israel had to learn what it truly meant to be the people of God.

The period in the wilderness was thus not an inconvenient and purposeless delay to the entry of the people of God into their promised homeland. It was a period of formation in which they were reshaped into a new people, aware of their privileges and responsibilities as those whom God had called. The Christian life, in the same way, is not a tedious and unimportant interlude between coming to know Christ and going to be with Christ. It is a time of spiritual development, in which we learn what it means to know Christ and how this affects every aspect of our lives.

The Promised Land lies ahead for us, as it did for Israel. From time to time we can catch a glimpse of its distant mountains gracing the horizon or hear an echo of its music. We must press on, travelling in hope and confidence, knowing that this land awaits us and that our Saviour accompanies us on the road that leads there. At times, we will feel lonely on that road, especially when the journey tires and discourages us. At these moments, we must remember three things.

First, we must realise that others are making this journey now, as many have made it before them. It may seem as if we are on our own, but this is not so. We are surrounded by a 'cloud of witnesses' (Hebrews 12:1–2) who have made this journey before us and who eagerly wait for us to join them. The great amphitheatre of life which surrounds us is packed with those who have already crossed the Jordan and entered the Promised Land, who are standing on their feet, cheering us on as we struggle to complete the journey from which they now rest.

You may *feel* that you are on your own. But open your eyes. See the marks of those who have been there before you. Their tracks lie ahead of you. The road on which you travel has been graced with their footsteps, as they sought to follow the Christ who has already made that journey and who awaits us on the other side. Hear the roar of encouragement from those distant mountains, and see beyond their peaks to the green and fragrant pastures which await you.

Second, we must accept that times of solitude can be used positively. Jesus regularly withdrew to be on his own. Why? To isolate himself from everything that distracts, in order that he might pray more effectively. Solitude deprives us of distractions and allows us to focus down on what really matters. Sometimes solitude is forced upon us; sometimes it is something that we choose. In either case, we can use it positively and effectively, as a time to be alone with Christ. Its eerie silence allows us to hear a gentle knocking at our door (Revelation 3:20). Every moment of solitude is potentially a moment of refreshment and renewal. In order for us to be of use to Christ in the world, we will need to withdraw from that world, in order to recharge our spiritual batteries and gain a new vision of how we might serve him.

Countless pastors could tell of how important solitude can be to their ministries. It allows them time to build a vision of their work and to allow themselves to be challenged and affirmed by the Lord they are trying to serve. John R. W. Stott, one of England's best-known pastors and writers of the twentieth century, found that such a time of solitude allowed him to sustain a highly pressurised and important ministry at All Souls Church, Langham Place, in the centre of London:

I have discovered the immense profit of a quiet day at least once a month. I learned this from the Revd L. F. E. Wilkinson during an address he gave at the Islington Clerical Conference in about 1951. It is the only thing I remember from the whole conference. But it came to me as a message from God. I had been precipitated into being Rector of All Souls at the age of twenty-nine, when I was much too young and inexperienced for such a responsibility. I began living from hand to mouth. Everything piled up and got on top of me. I felt crushed by the heavy administrative load. I started having the typical clerical nightmare: I was halfway up the pulpit steps when I realised that I had forgotten to prepare a sermon. Then came L. F. E. Wilkinson's address. 'Take a quiet day once a month,' he said, or words to that effect. 'Go away into the country, if you can, where you can be sure of being undisturbed. Stand back, look ahead, and consider where you are going. Allow yourself to be caught up into the mind and the perspective of God. Try to see things as he sees them. Relax!' I did. I went home, and immediately marked one day a month in my engagement book with the letter 'Q' for Quiet. And as I began to enjoy these days, the intolerable burden lifted and has never returned . . . I could not exaggerate the blessing which these quiet days have brought to my life and ministry.[9]

Solitude is loneliness seen positively. We may rejoice when with company, as we share friendship and fellowship. We may rejoice when we are on our own, because we can avoid distractions and can thus reflect and pray more effectively. It is in these moments that we appreciate the truth in those wise words: 'Be still, and know that I am God' (Psalm 46:10). In such quiet moments, we can entrust everything to our Lord and learn to see things from his perspective.

Finally, remember that the Christ who died for you and who called you has not abandoned you. He has promised that he is 'the way, the truth and the life' (John 14:6). Christ does not point us ahead, then leave us alone to make the journey on our own or in our own strength. Martin Luther (1483–1546) made this point powerfully when he asked the readers of this verse to hear Christ speaking these words to them:

Think of nothing but these words of mine: 'I am the Way.' So make sure that you tread on me, that is, that you cling to me with a strong faith and great confidence. I will be the bridge which will carry you across. You will pass over from death and the fear of hell into the life which awaits you. For I paved that way for you. I walked across it myself, so that I might take you and all my people across. All that you need do is place your feet confidently upon me.[10]

If you feel lonely, use your imagination to bring these words of Luther to life. Let them be like living water to you, as you realise that the road on which you set your feet has been paved by Christ. He is the bridge which will take you over the Jordan into that Promised Land where countless others await you, to greet your safe return to your homeland.

Horatius Bonar (1808–89), one of Scotland's leading nineteenth-century pastors and hymn-writers, is perhaps best known for his hymns 'Fill thou my life, O Lord my God' and 'I heard the voice of Jesus say'. Yet he was also someone who gave great thought to the question of how we could sustain our faith in moments of darkness and loneliness – moments which he knew well from his own life and ministry. His thoughts on this matter form a fitting conclusion to this section.

We are but as wayfaring men, wandering in the lonely night, who see dimly upon the distant mountain peak the reflection of a sun that never rises here, but which shall never set in the 'new heavens' thereafter. And this is enough. It comforts and cheers us on our dark and rugged way.[11]

6

Knowing Christ in anxiety

We are all familiar with the Gospel story of the disciples' terror at being engulfed by a strong wind as they crossed the Sea of Galilee on their way to Capernaum (John 6:16–21). They seemed to be at the mercy of the elements and were deeply afraid. Then, at the height of the storm, Jesus appeared and spoke these words to them: 'It is I. Do not be afraid.'

The words spoken by Jesus are both consoling and challenging. Yet the traditional translation of those words is not quite accurate, nor is it adequate to convey the full import of Christ's meaning. A better translation would read like this: 'I am. Do not be afraid.' The very presence of Christ is itself enough to calm our storms and assuage our fears. *Christ is here*. This is a promise nestling within a statement. We should not be afraid, for Christ is with us. This incident illustrates the importance of Christ as a consoling presence. Others stress his importance as a solid foundation, a rock upon which we may build and in which we may trust in times of difficulty or danger.

So what are we afraid of? In what situations might we need to rediscover and draw upon the consolation of the assured presence of Christ amid the storms of our lives? In some ways, this is a very personal question, in that we have anxieties about many different things. However, the same principle holds: we need to hand over our anxieties to the living Christ and trust him for all that lies ahead.

Some are anxious about the *future*. How can we know what we should be doing for God? Might we not end up doing something which wastes our talents – or worse, which accidentally takes us away from the path that God has planned for us? It is so difficult to be sure about these things, yet they are so important. It is no wonder that so many are anxious about the future. So much seems to be at stake. And so we lie awake at night, worrying. The peace which Christ promises to those who know him seems to have passed us by.

Something is wrong here. One of the great themes that Paul develops in his letter to the Philippians is that of Christian tranquillity – being able to experience the peace of Christ in a troubled and uncertain world.

I have learned, in whatever state I am, to be content. I know how to be abased, and I know how to abound; in any and all circumstances I have learned the secret of facing plenty and hunger, abundance and want. I can do all things in him who strengthens me.

(Philippians 4:11–13)

So why are we so anxious about the present or future? Do we not know that, whatever the future holds and wherever it may take us, we may have the consoling presence of Christ as we travel? What is the problem?

One obvious answer is that we fear complacency. It is a good answer, in so many ways. We always need to ask whether we could be achieving more for Christ, just as we must keep our spiritual health continually under review. Complacency is a real barrier to growing to know Christ better. Yet, on reflection, this is not the real issue at stake here. Anxiety cannot be equated with a lack of *complacency*. When all is said and done, anxiety is fundamentally a lack of *trust*. We refuse to trust that our futures lie securely in God's hands. Perhaps believing that God needs prompting or assisting in some way, we go ahead and develop our own visions of the future and pursue our own agendas. And underlying this is the most fundamental of all sins – a lack of trust in the God who created and redeemed us.

It is here that we need to entrust our futures to Christ. We must hand over the future, and our anxieties concerning it, to him. Few are privileged to know exactly what the Lord wants them to do with their lives. Some find discernment a very difficult business, in that we are confronted with so many options for our futures. Which shall we choose? Others seem to have relatively few possibilities available to them. From a human viewpoint – but *not* from God's perspective! – they seem to have much less to offer. Both need to learn that the Lord is able to take and bless whatever we do as we seek to serve him. In whatever walk of life we find ourselves, the Lord will be able to use us to serve him. Remember that Paul opens his letter to the Philippians by reminding them that he is in prison for Christ. Yet even in that apparently unpromising situation, he has found that he can serve his Lord and bear witness to his faith and to his Saviour (Philippians 1:12–14). It is important to be distrustful of human estimations of careers and situations. What matters from God's perspective is not the status of our position, but the opportunities it brings for service and proclamation of the gospel.

In his *Self-Abandonment to Divine Providence,* Jean-Pierre de Caussade (1675–1751) writes of a 'dynamic surrender to the will and way of God'. The rich and helpful phrase 'dynamic surrender' points to our need to unreservedly entrust ourselves to divine providence. De Caussade sees this surrender as an active and purposeful decision on the part of the human will. It involves the deliberate decision on our part to submit ourselves totally to God, who may then be relied upon to bring about the good that he wills for us. We must actively seek and discern the will of God, and then gladly submit to it.

We must surrender and abandon ourselves to his divine will in perfect confidence. This divine will is infinitely wise, powerful and benevolent towards those who completely and unreservedly place their hope in it, who love and seek it alone, and who believe with an unshakeable faith and confidence that what it effects in us at each moment is indeed the best.[12]

When I first read those words, I was thrilled. Here was someone who really believed in the goodness and graciousness of a God who guides! The words reassured me, but they also challenged me. Why did I not do the same thing? Why was I worried about the future when I ought to be using that same mental energy to explore how I could serve God better, in whatever situations he placed me?

So trust that God can use you, wherever you find yourself. And pray about where he might want you to be and what he might want you to do, perhaps allowing biblical passages to guide your thinking. But be careful! A geographically challenged friend of a colleague of mine spent some time as a missionary in Israel. I asked him why. 'Well,' he said, 'I wasn't sure where I should go as a missionary. So I decided to read through the Old Testament, looking for guidance. And, you know, just about every page seemed to talk about this place called "Israel". So I guess that's where the Lord wanted me to be.'

Some are anxious about *failure*. We hold back from attempting anything for Christ, because we fear that we shall fail. Part of our concern is that we do not wish to dishonour Christ. Yet perhaps a greater part of that concern relates to our anxiety about not wishing to be seen to fail. We fear that our status in the sight of others might be compromised by failure.

It is important to name these anxieties, just as it is equally important to respond to them. Becoming aware of the precise nature of our worries is the first stage in dealing with the threat they pose to our walk with Christ. Part of the great venture of the Christian life is a willingness to take faithful risks – to step out in faith, believing that some particular project needs to be undertaken. Paul urged us to put everything to the test (1 Thessalonians 5:21), so that part of our ministry of discernment is testing both present and future possibilities. Gideon put out a fleece to test the Lord's will (Judges 6:36–40); in our case, the fleece in question may be to begin a possible ministry or course of action and see if the Lord blesses it. If it seems that this will not be blessed, we should not think of it in human terms as a 'failure' but as a faithful and obedient attempt to discern the Lord's will in this situation.

Yet failure – real failure – can have a powerful and positive spiritual impact. Many pastors will tell how their ministries first came alive after a pastoral failure, when they were forced to re-evaluate themselves. Often, they came to the conclusion that their ministries had been based upon their own strengths. They had learned to trust in their own resources and abilities, and had come to believe that their success was their own personal achievement. They *needed* to be humbled, and to learn to trust in God rather than in their own wisdom and strength. Our personal failures can easily become the gateways to spiritual growth – provided we seize the opportunity they offer and allow them to teach us.

Some are anxious about their *weakness*. How can we cope with all the challenges that are thrown at us? How can the Lord make any use of what seem to us to be very slender and fragile gifts? What happens if people ask us questions about our faith at work? Here we need to learn to trust Christ. It is his gospel, and he delights in using weak and frail creatures in his service. We need to learn that it is not who we are, or even what we are, that matters to Christ in this respect. *It is what we allow him to do in and through us.* We must trust that Christ will be able to make use of what we can offer. In short: we must do our best – and let Christ do the rest.

Our anxiety here arises partly because we fear that we cannot even begin to do for Christ what he has done for us. We know that we shall fall short. We know the immensity of the tasks that need to be done, and feel that we cannot possibly meet the exceedingly great standards of excellence that he has a right to expect from us. Now let us be clear that we do indeed need to strive towards giving our utmost for Christ. Yet he is able to take and use whatever we can give him. The one who took a few loaves and fishes to feed the multitude can also take the lowly offerings we can make and do great and wonderful things with them. We need to trust totally that Christ can use us, despite our weakness and frailty.

I learned this the hard way. About fifteen years ago, I was asked by a colleague to take a service for him in the chapel of Jesus College, Oxford, during the summer vacation when he would be away on holiday with his family. An international summer school was taking place in the college, and its organisers had indicated that they would like to end the conference with a service in the college chapel. Having been assured that this involved little more than the reading of prayers and announcing of hymns, I gladly undertook to help my colleague out in this small way.

On the day appointed for the service, I duly turned up. There were about fifty people in the chapel, and printed Orders of Service had been liberally distributed on every seat. I checked quickly to make sure that the hymns to be sung were those which had been agreed with the college organist. Reassured that they were, I relaxed. The service got under way and seemed to be going well.

It was after the third hymn that things began to go wrong. We sang that hymn with great enthusiasm. After it ended, a curious silence descended on the chapel. It was as if people were waiting for something to happen. I hurriedly checked the Order of Service again, and noticed two words which I seemed to have overlooked on my earlier – and, as events proved, rather too cursory – reading. The two words? 'The sermon'. After about ten seconds, it became clear that nobody else in the chapel was going to preach the sermon. I realised, with a sinking feeling, that there was a very simple explanation for this silence. The congregation was waiting for me to begin my sermon – a sermon I had not prepared. 'Let us pray,' I said. And I really meant it!

Having prepared nothing, I simply talked about the first two things that came into my head. The Church of England seems to have decided at some point back in the reign of Elizabeth I that every sermon should have three points, but I only had two thoughts that day, loosely based upon the readings earlier in the service. I set them out as clearly as I could, and hoped that nobody would notice that they had been thrown together at a few seconds' notice. After I had finished, we sang our final hymn and the congregation departed. If they noticed that the sermon was less than polished, they were far too polite to mention it.

A week later, I received two letters from people in that congregation who had now returned to North America. My first correspondent informed me that the first point I had made had spoken to him very deeply, and he had now decided to become a Christian as a result. The other letter told a similar story; this time, however, it was the second point which had proved so decisive.

Part of me felt ashamed at these letters. How could a sermon thrown together at a moment's notice have such an effect? I normally prepare sermons *months* in advance. Yet none of these well-crafted sermons seemed ever to have had quite such an impact. Maybe I should give up preparing them properly? But the true lesson I learned was as simple as it is reassuring. When you fall back on the graciousness of our Lord, he honours our cries for help. The two ideas I had were not my own; they just flew into my mind as if someone had turned on a light or flashed them up on a screen. And they were the right two ideas.

The way in which knowing Christ enables us to deal with such doubts and anxieties naturally leads us on to consider the issue of doubt itself.

7

Knowing Christ in doubt

Doubt is a perennial problem in the life of faith. Doubt reflects our inability to be absolutely certain about what we believe. As Paul reminds us, we walk by faith, not by sight (2 Corinthians 5:7), which has the inevitable result that we cannot prove every aspect of our faith. This should not disturb us too much. After all, what is there in life that we can be absolutely certain about? We can be sure that $2 + 2 = 4$, but that is hardly going to change our lives. The simple fact of life is that everything worth believing in goes beyond what we can be absolutely sure about. Can I be sure that God loves me? Or that democracy is to be preferred to fascism?

In part, doubt reflects the continued presence and power of sin within us, reminding us of our need for grace and preventing us from becoming complacent about our relationship with God. We are all sinners, and we all suffer from doubt, to a greater or lesser extent. Our relationship with God is something we need to work at, conscious that in doing so we are working with God and not on our own (Philippians 2:12–13). Sin causes us to challenge the promises of God, to mistrust him. A careful reading of Genesis 3:1–5 makes it clear that mistrust of God is the ultimate 'original sin'.

Sin can be thought of as a personal force in our lives which aims to separate us from God. It is only by causing us to turn away from God that sin can gain or regain a hold over us. Faith is not just a willingness and ability to trust in God; it is the channel through which his grace flows to us. It is our lifeline to God. It is like the trunk of a tree, transferring life-giving sap from its roots to its branches; it both supports and nourishes their growth. Break that link, and the branches wither (John 15:1–8). If sin can be thought of as possessing any strategy, it is to break that link, to deny us access to the promises and power of God, and thus to allow itself to regain its former hold over our lives.

Doubt is also a reflection of human frailty. The severe limitations placed upon human capacities by the fact that we are creatures, not God, has been a major theme of Christian theology down the centuries. Thomas Aquinas, writing in the thirteenth century, stressed that God was obliged to speak to us using images and analogies. Our created and finite minds are simply not vast enough to comprehend God. We cannot fully comprehend God and his ways. Knowing that this is the case – for, after all, he created us – God reveals himself up to the limits of our abilities. This reflects a limitation on our part, not on God's. John Calvin put the point at issue like this: 'God accommodates himself to our abilities.' In other words, God knows our limitations and adapts himself accordingly.

Our limitations as God's fallen and fallible creatures prevent us from seeing things as clearly as we would like. Suppose that I want to see the stars during the hours of daylight. The simple fact of the matter is that the human eye cannot achieve this in broad daylight. It is only when darkness falls that the faint light of the stars stands out against the darkness of the night sky. The stars are still there during daylight; it is just that the human eye cannot discern their presence.

When night falls, however, the brilliance of the sun disappears, and our eyes adjust to allow us to see the tiny pinpoints of stellar light coming from the depths of our universe, highlighted against the blackness of the night. The stars do not need darkness to exist; we, on the other hand, need precisely that darkness if we are to see them and convince ourselves that they are there. So it is with God. Just as our eyes cannot see the stars during the day, so our minds simply cannot take in the fulness of God. Being human places limits on what we can see, know and understand. Being prepared to accept these limitations is an essential part of growing in faith.

Doubt, then, results partly from the simple fact that we are created, finite and fallen and are unable to discern the 'big picture' of the workings of God in the world. Yet it is not doubt in general but certain specific doubts which trouble many Christians in their personal walk of faith. One of them can be stated like this: How can Christ really love me? If he knew what I was really like, he would probably want nothing to do with me. This doubt has caused considerable distress to many Christians, especially those who are intensely aware of their own sinfulness. So often, we feel that Christ can only love us if he ignores our sin, or pretends that we are not really sinners after all. Experience, conscience and faith seem to be seriously out of step here. How can God love people like us?

Much the same point is made by Paul in his reflections on the meaning of the death of Christ. It is, he suggests, perfectly conceivable to imagine circumstances under which you might give your life for somebody else – provided, of course, that it was somebody rather splendid, a really good person. Even then, however, it would still be unusual for someone to willingly give up their life for another person. Yet God demonstrates his love for us, in that Christ died for us while we were still sinners (Romans 5:6–8). What on earth would he do that for? Why should God love sinners so much? Even before we got round to repenting, God loved us. Amazingly, God loved us long before we loved him (1 John 4:10–11).

Our disbelief that Christ should love us ultimately rests upon our feeling that his love must depend on our attractiveness. We find it difficult to see anything special about ourselves that should merit so astonishing and so loving a response from our Saviour. Yet Christ's love for us ultimately rests not on our merits, but on his own character as a loving and compassionate Saviour. The cross of Christ expresses the nature and the full extent of his tender love for us, reassuring us that we are precious in his sight. How often has it been said that 'Beauty is in the eye of the beholder'? Why should Christ see us as worthy of his love? Not on account of anything which we have done, or anything which we are – but on account of what Christ is like and what he has done for us through his incarnation, death and resurrection.

Most of us feel deeply unworthy of the love of God, on account of our selfishness and guilt. Sin affects us profoundly in what we think, say and do. It makes us tend to be sceptical about God, disobedient to him and reluctant to trust him. Yet God is able to distinguish between sin and the sinner. Sin is like a force which holds us in captivity against our will; God sees us as captives, struggling to escape, and takes pity upon us. It is like corrosion, which distorts the image of God within us; God anticipates the renewal and restoration of that image. Sin is like a wound, which disfigures us; God looks forward to the time when we shall, through his grace, be healed. Sin is like a layer of dirt or corrosion, which makes us seem unattractive and unbecoming; God sees us as washed clean through the blood of Christ, our beauty restored to what it was on the first morning of creation.

In the late fifteenth century, the Florentine sculptor Agostino d'Antonio began work on a huge block of marble with a view to producing a spectacular sculpture. After a few attempts to make something out of it, he gave it up as worthless. The block of marble – now badly disfigured – lay idle for forty years. Then Michelangelo took an interest in it. He saw beyond the ugly disfigured block of marble to the magnificent artistic creation he knew he could achieve with it. As a result, he began work. The final statue – the celebrated *David* – is widely regarded as one of the most outstanding artistic achievements of all time.

Michelangelo was able to see beyond the unpromising exterior of the block of marble to what he could eventually make of it. Similarly, God is able to see beyond our sinful predicament and all its consequences, knowing what he will be able to do with us through breaking the power of sin and restoring us to his image and likeness. Within each of us, the image of God (Genesis 1:26–7) is to be found, however disfigured and corrupted by sin it may presently be. God is able to recover this image through grace, as we are conformed to Christ. Just as the figure of David lay hidden within the marble, discernible only to the eye of its creator, so the image of God (however tarnished by sin) lies within us, seen and known by God himself. Yet God loves us while we are still sinners. Acceptance of that love of God for us is a major step along the road which leads to our liberation from the tyranny of sin.

One of the finest reflections on this question comes from a hymn composed by Charlotte Elliot (1789–1871), who was deeply troubled by a series of doubts concerning her personal worthiness to receive Christ as her Saviour. After a conversation with a visiting pastor in 1822, she realised that she need not fear her personal unworthiness. Her grounds of acceptance lay in the fact that Christ had bid her come to him, knowing her as she was. His saving death availed for her and broke down every barrier between her and her Saviour. Fourteen years later, she penned this hymn, partly to express her own feelings of reassurance and partly to console and encourage others. I continue to find this hymn immensely insightful and reassuring, and often dwell on its words as I seek to know Christ more fully.

> Just as I am, without one plea,
> But that Thy blood was shed for me,
> And that Thou bidd'st me come to Thee,
> O Lamb of God, I come.

Just as I am, and waiting not
To rid my soul of one dark blot,
To Thee whose blood can cleanse each spot,
O Lamb of God, I come, I come.

Just as I am, Thy love unknown
Has broken ev'ry barrier down;
Now to be Thine, yea, Thine alone,
O Lamb of God, I come.

Just as I am, tho' tossed about
With many a conflict, many a doubt,
Fightings and fears within, without,
O Lamb of God, I come.

Just as I am, poor, wretched, blind —
Sight, riches, healing of the mind,
Yea, all I need in Thee to find —
O Lamb of God, I come.

Just as I am, Thou wilt receive,
Wilt welcome, pardon, cleanse, relieve,
Because Thy promise I believe,
O Lamb of God, I come![13]

As can be seen from this hymn, our difficulty in accepting that Christ loves us arises partly from a sense of sin. Probably the greatest paradox of Christian spirituality is this: the closer we draw to Christ, the more conscious we become of our sin. The radiance of his glory shows us up as wretched, weak, stained and lost. The more clearly we discern the face of Christ, the more we become aware of our failures and the pain which they must cause him. An increasing awareness of sin can thus be a sign of growing *closer* to Christ, rather than of moving away from him. The closer we draw, the more his radiance exposes our sin, failures and blemishes.

So how can we be reassured of the love of Christ for us? Perhaps one of the most helpful ways of doing this is to reflect on the image of the dying Christ, stretched out on the cross for us. It is here that the importance of our theme of 'knowing Christ' becomes so important. Use your imagination to build up a mental picture of the scene. Or search your library or surf the internet for some paintings of the scene, such as those which have become classics in the history of art. Perhaps you could read one of the four passion narratives (Matthew 27:11–65; Mark 15; Luke 23; John 18:28–19:42), and picture the events of that first Good Friday. Think carefully of the loneliness, of the pain, of the suffering, of the sense of hopelessness and helplessness of the scene. Think of that sad and dignified face, contorted with pain. Let the full horror of that scene impress itself on your mind. And all of this because God loved you, and gave his only Son for you.

For many Christians, one of the most powerful ways of recalling this scene and understanding its relevance for us is to share in a communion service. The bread and the wine are visible, tangible reminders of that scene. They represent the sufferings of Christ. They are 'dear tokens of his passion' (Charles Wesley). And as you eat and drink the bread and wine, you are being reminded of the enormous cost of your redemption, of how much you must matter to God if he went to such lengths to find you. Let them act as triggers to your memory, starting off trains of thought which converge on the crucifixion of the Lord. 'This is love: not that we loved God but that he loved us and sent his Son as an atoning sacrifice for our sins' (1 John 4:10).

It is in moments of doubt that we need to draw close to Christ, and allow him to draw close to us. One area of the Christian life in which this is especially significant is the issue of suffering, to which we now turn.

8

Knowing Christ in suffering

I have never suffered to any significant extent, so write this section with a certain degree of hesitation. Others are far better qualified than I to write this, and would speak with a degree of integrity which I cannot match. I write on the theme, however, as one who believes passionately that knowing Christ will be an immense consolation to me when I am called upon to suffer. The present section is what I would like someone to say to me when that moment comes.

To know Christ is to know a compassionate God. Paul opens one of his most reflective letters with a reflection on the themes of human suffering and divine consolation:

> Praise be to the God and Father of our Lord Jesus Christ, the Father of compassion and the God of all comfort, who comforts us in all our troubles, so that we can comfort those in any trouble with the comfort we ourselves have received from God. For just as the sufferings of Christ flow over into our lives, so also through Christ our comfort overflows.
>
> (2 Corinthians 1:3–5, NIV)

God is *compassionate*. The suffering of the world affects God. It grieves him. The pages of history are stained with the tears of our compassionate God.

The word 'compassionate', like 'sympathetic', has the basic meaning of 'suffering alongside someone', and thus possesses extended meanings such as 'kindness', 'consideration' or 'clemency'. To be compassionate or sympathetic in the full sense of these words is to be able to set yourself alongside one who is suffering, opening yourself to them to the extent that you share their pain and anguish. Christ is our sympathetic high priest (Hebrews 4:15). He has been through all that we are being asked to go through. Knowing this, we may approach him with confidence. Why? Because Christ understands our plight. More than that: he has *shared* it; he has been there, and thus created a powerful bond of sympathy between himself and ourselves.

The face of the crucified Christ, shot through with pain and tears, allows us to grasp something of how God must feel over the way his creation is groaning in pain as it awaits its liberation from bondage to decay (Romans 8:20–2). To know Christ is to know the father-heart of a God who chooses to suffer along with those whom he created and loves. In his love for us, God consoles us in our suffering.

I often find myself thinking here of one of the great prophetic passages of the Old Testament – the prophecy of the Suffering Servant of God (Isaiah 52:13–53:12). It is impossible to read this passage without being reminded of the last hours of the life of Christ. Suffering, shame and pain cast their shadow over the entire section. The passage appears to open with the theme of exaltation: 'See, my servant shall prosper; he shall be exalted and lifted up, and shall be very high' (Isaiah 52:13). This might suggest that this servant of God will find fame, fortune and favour in life. But soon the darker side of the theme becomes clear. Christ is indeed exalted and lifted up – but he is lifted up on the cross at Calvary, for all to see and despise, in the most public and painful form of execution. 'I, when I am lifted up from the earth, will draw all people to myself' (John 12:32).

The themes of rejection, being reviled and undergoing suffering now come to the fore. 'He was despised and rejected by others; a man of suffering and acquainted with infirmity' (Isaiah 53:3). The Suffering Servant shares our human situation, drinking deeply of the bitter waters of pain and affliction. The poignancy of the passage is unmistakable. It sketches, briefly and yet with great effect, the image of a tender young life destroyed through suffering.

Almost anticipating such a development, the passage moves on to reflect on the purpose of this innocent suffering:

> Surely he has borne our infirmities and carried our diseases; yet we accounted him stricken, struck down by God, and afflicted. But he was wounded for our transgressions, crushed for our iniquities; upon him was the punishment that made us whole, and by his bruises we are healed.
>
> (Isaiah 53:4–5)

The first statement here is astonishing, and pulls us up short. The Servant is suffering, not on behalf of himself, but for us. But how? And why? The Servant has the sorrow of a sinful world laid upon his shoulders, in much the same way as the priest laid the sins of his people upon the scapegoat, before driving it into the wilderness.

In some way, the Servant has taken upon himself the burden of our grief and sorrow. Those looking on rush to the wrong conclusion, believing that he has been condemned by God. But subsequent events make it clear that this is not the case. In some way, it is *we* who have been condemned, and the Suffering Servant who bears our punishment. Suffering has been taken away from us and laid upon him. Through the mystery of God's compassion and care, the Servant is prepared to suffer in order that others might be thought of as being righteous (53:11). He is content to be treated as if he were a sinner, bearing their sin, and suffering beside them (53:12).

This passage, perhaps more powerfully than any other, brings out the idea of the compassion of Christ. He is prepared to suffer alongside sinners, being reckoned among their number. There were three crosses at Calvary. When Christ was crucified, they executed a convicted criminal on either side of him. Of the four evangelists, it is Luke who especially draws our attention to the full significance of this point. Jesus was utterly innocent of any crime; indeed, one of the two criminals, astonished that Jesus was being executed with them, turned to the other, and said: 'We indeed have been condemned justly, for we are getting what we deserve for our deeds, but this man has done nothing wrong' (Luke 23:41). Furthermore, the officer in charge of the execution squad, astonished at the events unfolding before his eyes, declared, 'Certainly this man was innocent' (Luke 23:47).

Jesus died between two criminals, sinners in the eyes of the world: 'they crucified Jesus there with the criminals, one on his right and one on his left' (Luke 23:33). What more dramatic symbol could one want of the compassion of Christ, when he suffered alongside sinners? Christ was present with those who suffered and finally died.

This is compassion in the full sense of the word. Here we see Jesus being prepared to suffer with sinners, being counted as if he were among their number and condemned to share their fate. And he accepted this identification, without any attempt to evade its consequences. He identified with us right up to the end, joining us in this solidarity of suffering.

To know Christ is to know a God who has gladly and willingly borne our sorrows on the bitter cross of Calvary. He became personally acquainted with our grief. God has shared our sufferings, injecting the fragrance of his redeeming presence into the darker side of our existence. God is a fellow-sufferer who understands, not someone who views our situation from a safe distance, uncomprehending and unaffected.

As I have deepened my familiarity with Christian literature over the years, I have noticed how some of the finest writings of faith have their origins in times of great suffering and trial. These 'songs of the night' speak of the reality of suffering, while at the same time affirming the steadfastness of the love of Christ in these times of darkness and sadness. One story that I found especially moving concerned Horatio G. Spafford, a Chicago lawyer whose family was deeply affected by the revivalist preaching of D. L. Moody. In November 1873, Spafford's wife and four daughters set off on the *Ville du Havre* to sail to France. Spafford had originally intended to sail with them but had to delay his plans due to work pressures. He would follow by the next available ship. The *Ville du Havre* collided with another ship and sank. Spafford's wife survived; his daughters perished. From that great sense of tragedy and loss sprang a hymn, which Spafford is said to have composed several months later after travelling to the site of the sinking of the *Ville du Havre* and the loss of his daughters. It has often seemed to me that it is in the darkness of the night that the light of faith is strongest.

> When peace, like a river, attendeth my way,
> When sorrows like sea billows roll;
> Whatever my lot, Thou hast taught me to say,
> It is well, it is well with my soul.
> It is well with my soul,
> It is well, it is well with my soul.
>
> Though Satan should buffet, tho' trials should come,
> Let this blest assurance control,
> That Christ has regarded my helpless estate,
> And hath shed His own blood for my soul.
> It is well with my soul,
> It is well, it is well with my soul.
>
> My sin – oh, the bliss of this glorious thought:
> My sin, not in part, but the whole –
> Is nailed to the cross and I bear it no more,

Praise the Lord, praise the Lord, O my soul!
It is well with my soul,
It is well, it is well with my soul.

And, Lord, haste the day when the faith shall be sight,
The clouds be rolled back as a scroll,
The trump shall resound and the Lord shall descend,
Even so, it is well with my soul.
It is well with my soul,
It is well, it is well with my soul.[14]

So how do such thoughts help us to cope with suffering? The key theme here is that of the compassion of Christ in our suffering. He knows what we are going through; he understands. The way of suffering has been graced by our creator and Saviour, whose hands reach out to uphold and embrace us in our shared pain. To know Christ is to have the privilege of sharing in the fellowship of his sufferings, knowing that we shall one day share in his glorious resurrection.

And how does this hope console us? It sets our present situation in its full context, by allowing eternity to break into time and illuminate it. Meditating on the sufferings and resurrection of Christ reminds and reassures us that 'our present sufferings are not worth comparing with the glory that will be revealed in us' (Romans 8:18, NIV). So are we frightened by death? Faith assures us that to die is to gain, and to be with the Christ we long to know fully. Are we troubled by sorrow? Faith tells us of another country – which is to be *our* country – where sorrow is no more, and where all tears have been wiped away. Do we suffer? Faith tells us of a time when death shall be swallowed up in victory, and the sufferings of the present day will seem insignificant in comparison with the joy that awaits us.

Just as suffering is real, so are the promises of God and the hope of eternal life. The death and resurrection of Christ, linked with the giving of the Holy Spirit, are pledges, sureties and guarantees that what has been promised to us will one day be brought to glorious realisation. For the moment we struggle and suffer in sadness mingled with bewilderment. But, one day, all that will be changed for the people of God:

> [God] will dwell with them as their God; they will be his peoples, and God himself will be with them: he will wipe every tear from their eyes. Death will be no more; mourning and crying and pain will be no more, for the first things have passed away.
>
> (Revelation 21:3–4)

In that hope, we go forward into life in faith. We may not know exactly where that faith will lead us. But we do know that, wherever we go, the God of all compassion goes ahead of us and journeys with us, consoling and reassuring us, until that day when we shall see him face to face, and know him as he knows us. To know Christ is to have the assurance that another country beckons us, as the Promised Land beckoned to Israel in the wilderness. Christ is the ground and guarantor that joy and glory lie on the far side of suffering. To know him is to anticipate passing through the valley of the shadow of death into the light of his presence.

PART 3

Knowing Christ through his encounters

The Gospels tell us of the encounters of Jesus and the transformation this brought to the lives of tired, confused, rejected and wounded people. People like me, who understand their faith primarily in terms of ideas, tend to concentrate on the teachings of Jesus and neglect his encounters. It is certainly true that Jesus teaches with the authority of God. Christ, the Christian faith affirms, is God incarnate, and thus speaks with the voice of God. Yet if we believe in the doctrine of the incarnation, we must go one step further than this. The Word of God became flesh, not merely so that it might be communicated to us, but so that it might encounter, challenge and embrace us. Every biblical encounter with Christ is of relevance to our present encounter with him, inviting us to go deeper and to know him better.

We shall be considering four classic encounters in this section, and asking how they can help deepen our personal encounter with Christ. To begin to appreciate the importance of such encounters, however, we may consider one as a model. This is the famous encounter between Christ and Zacchaeus. Luke opens the story by telling of how Christ visited the city of Jericho:

He entered Jericho and was passing through it. A man was there named Zacchaeus; he was a chief tax collector and was rich. He was trying to see who Jesus was, but on account of the crowd he could not, because he was short in stature. So he ran ahead and climbed a sycamore tree to see him, because he was going to pass that way. When Jesus came to the place, he looked up and said to him, 'Zacchaeus, hurry and come down: for I must stay at your house today.' So he hurried down and was happy to welcome him. All who saw it began to grumble and said, 'He has gone to be the guest of one who is a sinner.' Zacchaeus stood there and said to the Lord, 'Look, half of my possessions, Lord, I will give to the poor; and if I have defrauded anybody of anything, I will pay back four times as much.' Then Jesus said to him, 'Today salvation has come to this house, because he too is a son of Abraham. For the Son of Man came to seek and to save the lost.'

(Luke 19:1–10)

Some have noticed how Jesus drew alongside people and urge us simply to do the same. 'Ministry is all about getting alongside people! It is about being available to them! There is no need to preach to them!' Yet we must be careful here. Christ's encounters with individuals were a means to an end – and the goal of those encounters was reconciliation with God and transformation of their lives. One of the means by which Christ encounters people today is through our witness to him. To be silent about Christ is to hinder others from learning of his encounter with us and sharing that life-changing experience.

Some people apparently confuse means and ends at this point, and suggest that simply drawing alongside people on the road of life is all that needs to be done as Christian service. The story of Zacchaeus helps us see that this is very inadequate. Christ encountered Zacchaeus; the result was repentance and personal transformation. Where there is no transformation of life, Christ has not been fully encountered.

Reflecting on the encounters of Christ serves to stimulate our imaginations and ensure that this aspect of our God-given identity is fully deployed in the process of knowing Christ. Reading of such an encounter allows us to picture it in the theatre of our minds. I find it helpful to close my eyes and hear the biblical account of Christ's encounters with others read aloud to me. As I hear the passage read out, I can begin to form my own mental picture of what happened. I can picture Zacchaeus trying to see Jesus, his short height preventing him from getting a good view of the man everyone is talking about. I can imagine him clambering up a nearby tree, and his embarrassment at being seen. And I can appreciate the astonishment that Zacchaeus must have felt when he heard Christ invite himself into his house.

Christ's encounters with individuals embody the gospel message. He accepts sinners and welcomes them into his presence, in the full knowledge that such a redemptive encounter must lead to personal transformation. In his actions and words, Christ affirms people through accepting them. Many academic theologians have made the point that Christ, in his personal ministry, embodies central themes of the gospel later stated in more theological terms by Paul – such as 'justification by faith' and 'salvation by grace'. Such doctrines risk becoming abstract ideas; in the ministry of Christ, however, they become living realities.

How can we *see* justification by faith? How can we represent this doctrine as the living sculpture of a changed life rather than an abstract concept? The answer is simple: we turn to the encounters of Christ with individuals, in which we see the words of the gospel proclamation made flesh in the everyday lives of those who met Christ.

Jesus is prepared to accept those whom the world regards as unacceptable. He sat at table with those the world regards as outcasts – such as tax collectors, the menial puppets of the Roman authorities. He mingled with those avoided by respectable people – such as prostitutes. He was seen alone with women

– a scandalous matter at the time – and talked to them as equals about the wonders of the kingdom of God (note the amazement of the disciples at this in John 4:27). He preached to Samaritans, to the horror of the Jews. He mingled with, spoke to and even touched lepers, who had been cast out by society as unclean (Mark 1:40–2), risking becoming leprous himself. (There is an obvious parallel with AIDS in our own day.) He ministered to senior Roman officers, looked upon with hatred and contempt by Jews, who saw them as oppressors. In short, Jesus was prepared to meet and accept even those whom society regarded as outcasts.

Again, we must emphasise that this acceptance is not an end in itself. It leads to the alteration of life. Perhaps the most striking example of this may be found in the story of Zacchaeus himself. He was a tax collector, viewed with utter contempt by his fellows. His low social status was compounded by the fact that he was small. With a few choice phrases, Luke persuades us that we are dealing with a man who was treated like dirt by society.

Yet Christ invited himself to Zacchaeus' house to share a meal. The enormously affirmative character of Christ's personal attitude towards the tax collector is evident from the joy with which Zacchaeus received him. And the story does not end there. Christ's affirmation of Zacchaeus led to his repentance. 'Look, half of my possessions, Lord, I will give to the poor; and if I have defrauded anybody of anything, I will pay back four times as much' (Luke 19:8). It was only then that Jesus declared that the restoration and healing was complete. 'Today salvation has come to this house' (Luke 19:9).

So what other encounters should we note? And what can we learn from them? In what follows, we shall consider four of the encounters which prepared the ground for knowing Christ more fully and more deeply. Although we stand in the shadows of these encounters, they illuminate our own relationship with Christ. In this life, we shall never share the privilege of any kind of direct, personal, physical encounter with Christ. Yet the four case studies which follow help us understand more of our own experience of the risen Christ, and prepare us for that day when we shall finally meet Christ face to face.

9

The fishermen by the sea

One of the earliest encounters to be reported in the Gospels concerns a small group of fishermen, struggling to make their living by the shores of Lake Galilee. The most terse and dramatic account of this incident is provided by Mark's Gospel:

> As Jesus passed along the Sea of Galilee, he saw Simon and his brother Andrew casting a net into the sea – for they were fishermen. And Jesus said to them, 'Follow me and I will make you fish for people.' And immediately they left their nets and followed him. As he went a little farther, he saw James son of Zebedee and his brother John, who were in their boat mending the nets. Immediately he called them; and they left their father Zebedee in the boat with the hired men, and followed him.
>
> (Mark 1:16–20)

Mark's breathtaking narrative – things happen 'immediately' – conveys a sense of speed and drama. There is something about Christ which compels an immediate and positive response.

The passage offers no reason for Simon's and Andrew's decision to follow him. It just happened. The same pattern is repeated with James and John. Christ looked into their eyes, and they saw something that eclipsed everything they had ever known up to this point. We find something like this reaction within the crowds that hear him speak: 'they were astounded at his teaching, for he taught them as one having authority' (Mark 1:22).

So what was it that made them leave everything behind, to follow Christ into the unknown? Christ calls them without offering them a vision for the future. He does not provide a business plan, nor a detailed account of what he proposes to do with them. He wants them, and he has a place for them. That is all they need to know. He *is* their future.

They could not help but be impressed by the attractiveness of the person of Christ. Everything that the fishermen knew, owned or longed for seemed insignificant in the light of the compelling personality which confronted them. They had yet to grasp just how important he was. There is no hint that they realised he was the Son of God incarnate upon this earth, or that they recognised him as Israel's long-awaited Messiah. Those insights would gradually dawn as they watched, listened and reflected. What they knew was that this was someone whose personality compelled them to leave all behind and follow him.

We are all in something like this position. When I made my decision to become a Christian, I thought I had gained a fairly good understanding of the importance of Christ. Yet as I look back on the series of footprints in my walk of faith, I realise how much I have developed since then. Our relationship with Christ is living and personal, and cries out to advance and develop. Realising that we must go further does not invalidate our earlier knowledge of Christ, or imply that we were not proper Christians at that time. The relationship with Christ was well and truly begun – but it had *only* begun. The walk of faith is a journey of advancement and discernment, in which we relate increasingly deeply and meaningfully to the one who has called us and made us his own.

Some begin by recognising Christ as teacher. That is good and true – in as far as it goes. But it is only part of the truth, and as such is inadequate. More remains to be discovered. One of the paradoxes of the Christian life is that it is only when one *has* gone deeper that one realises that one *needed* to go deeper. Part of our spiritual dilemma is that it is only when we have moved on a step in our devotional lives that we come to appreciate how much we needed to move on. 'I'm perfectly happy with what I have!' is a common response to a suggestion that people need to move on in their spiritual lives. Yet once they have moved on and realise how essential such a move was, we find a different response: 'How could I have been so blind? Or so arrogant? How could I have failed to see what I needed to do?' It is easy to be wise after the event.

So do you know Christ as your teacher? Excellent. Now you need to discover him as your Saviour. Do you know him as your friend? Excellent. Now you need to discover him as your Lord. Each advance in the Christian life builds on what is already present, yet leads us on to new vistas of divine grace and love. The disciples first discovered Christ as the one who commanded their attention and obedience. As they grew to know him more intimately, they discovered him to be the one who held their own destiny and that of the world in his hands. Too often, we constrict Christ, refusing to concede that there might be more to him than we know. It is time to allow him to expand our horizons, gently challenging us as to the adequacy of our current grasp of his significance for us, and for the world.

So how can we know Christ more profoundly? One of the ways that I have found most helpful is to allow others to tell me of how they encountered Christ and the impact which he has had on their lives. As I listen, I find two things happening. First, I come to know more about the person I am listening to. It is a way of developing the fellowship which I enjoy with them. But second, and more important, it allows me to grasp more of the 'boundless riches of Christ' (Ephesians 3:8), as I realise that others have often found riches in their appreciation of Christ that I have yet to discover, or have overlooked. There is a superfluity of significance in Christ, exceeding what any one person can ever hope to uncover. Every testimony we hear to Christ is thus potentially a challenge to go further in our own walk with him.

10

The woman at the well

William Inge (1860–1954), sometime dean of St Paul's Cathedral, London, was noted for his witty reflections on English church life during the 1920s. One of these concerns a telegram sent to a society wedding reception. The sender, perhaps being a little financially challenged, decided to send a biblical text by way of encouragement to the happy couple. His choice of text was admirable: 'perfect love casts out fear' (1 John 4:18). So the telegram was sent off. It read simply: '1 John 4:18'. Unfortunately, the post office clerk who transmitted the message was not used to dealing with biblical references and passed it on as 'John 4:18'. The telegram duly arrived at the wedding reception. A Bible was found, and the following text read to the newly married couple: 'The fact is, you have had five husbands, and the man you now have is not your husband.' This was *not* well received.

The fourth chapter of John's Gospel tells of an encounter between Christ and a Samaritan woman. The full significance of the dialogue is likely to be missed by modern readers, even though it is hinted at in the passage itself (see John 4:9, 27). In the first place, Christ was meeting with a Samaritan – and the Jews had long come to regard the Samaritans as untouchables. They were detested, and excluded from Jewish society. That is why the Parable of the Good Samaritan is so powerful and challenging: someone contemporary Jewish society regarded as an outcast fulfilled the requirements of the Old Testament law, where its official Jewish representatives failed to do so (Luke 10:30–7).

Yet the person with whom Christ gladly spent time was more than a Samaritan person; she was a Samaritan *woman*. The crude patriarchy of the time meant that it was considered inappropriate for a respectable male to have a meeting with a woman. Women were widely seen as the source of temptation and sin, and were shunned by reputable men. Part of the glory of the Christian gospel is the breaking down of such barriers and the full acceptance of women as equals with men in the kingdom of God – a theme gloriously affirmed by Paul: 'There is no longer Jew or Greek, there is no longer slave or free, there is no longer male and female; for all of you are one in Christ Jesus' (Galatians 3:28).

A double prejudice is thus confronted and overwhelmed. In this personal encounter, Christ models the life of the coming kingdom. Those who were reviled and excluded by the Jewish religious establishment would be welcomed into the kingdom. Paul sets out the theoretical basis of this in his letters; Christ models and embodies this in his dealings with individuals.

Christ does more than merely meet with this Samaritan woman. He takes her seriously, and engages in detailed conversation with her. Yet the real wonder of this encounter is not the breakdown of social barriers, nor the overcoming of the traditional prejudices of the period. The Samaritan woman does more than meet with a Jewish rabbi; she meets with the Saviour of the world, the Son of God incarnate. To begin with, the woman sees Christ as a kindly person who takes pity on her and condescends to speak to her; in reality, she is in the presence of the Son of God, who entered our world in order to meet and heal the wounded and broken human race. As the passage progresses, we find a remarkable deepening of insight. The woman initially sees a thirsty man; finally, she recognises him as the one who can meet her own deeper thirst for meaning and acceptance. She sees him as someone who, like her, is tired; gradually, she realises that he is the one who is able to refresh and renew others. She rushes back to her city to tell others of this remarkable person (John 4:28–9).

Is not this the inevitable result of a true encounter with Christ? That we long to tell others of what we have found? Or, better, *who* we have found? We find the same thing happening to Philip. After his encounter with Jesus (John 1:43), Philip is overwhelmed with wonder and excitement. He rushes to tell Nathanael, who is sceptical. 'Can anything good come out of Nazareth?' Philip does not waste time with wordy arguments. He wants Nathanael to experience the same encounter. His response is as simple as it is effective: 'Come and see' (John 1:46).

Perhaps Philip knew that he could never put into words the full wonder of his encounter with Christ. Perhaps he did not want to waste time arguing with Nathanael. Or perhaps he just knew that the encounter with the person of Christ would prove compelling. There is an important insight here concerning the nature of evangelism. Arguments doubtless have their place in our witness to Christ. Yet there is something more important – our willingness to point others to Christ as the source and wellspring of our faith. It is our task and our privilege to point others to the spring of living water from which they may drink deeply, and to tell them of the bread of life on which we have fed. In the end, the responsibility lies with them to 'taste and see that the Lord is good' (Psalm 34:8).

11

The doubter: Thomas

It is often hard to believe in the resurrection. Doubts often surface, reflecting our own feelings that perhaps the gospel is just too good to be true. There has to be a catch somewhere. Or maybe, because it all happened so long ago, we cannot really trust the Gospel accounts. They are wish-fulfilments, the dreams of people who long for a better world and are unable to cope with the harshness of the real world in which we live. There has been no shortage of those who want to ridicule the Christian faith, especially its celebration of the resurrection of Christ. It's all a children's story, we are told. It cannot be taken seriously.

Doubt is part of being human. We are frail, fallen and finite – and in each of these ways the quality of our faith is weakened. We long to see things from God's perspective. We yearn for the removal of the cloud of sin which causes us to doubt God's goodness and waver in our commitment. Yet we know that it is only when we stand in the New Jerusalem that our doubts will finally be thrown to one side. What we must do until that glorious day is to anticipate its coming, and begin to envisage what it will be like to live in the total trust and commitment which 'knowing Christ' properly entails.

When dealing with doubts at an earlier stage in my Christian life, I tended to offer rational justifications of my faith. The sort of arguments which I would bring to bear against critics of the resurrection would go like this:

- Some say that Christ just swooned on the cross, and that he later revived in the coolness of the tomb. The 'resurrection' was thus nothing more than a man who recovered from having fainted. But that makes little sense. The Roman soldiers knew what they were doing, and they would have made sure that Christ was dead before releasing the corpse for burial.

- Others say that the disciples fell victim to some kind of mass hysteria, in which they imagined the dead Christ to be restored to them. Yet this fails to even begin to do justice to the New Testament evidence. It is clear that the world of the disciples was completely transformed. What had been a band of demoralised people was utterly transformed into a dedicated and highly motivated team of evangelists who were perfectly prepared to be martyred for their beliefs. The resurrection of Christ provides the best explanation of this radical change in their behaviour.

These arguments are important. Yet their appeal was to my reason, rather than to my heart or imagination. If doubt were simply a matter of the mind, then this would not be the cause of any great problems. But there is more to doubt than intellectual difficulty. *Doubt is a matter of the heart, as much as the mind.* The encounter between Christ and Thomas demonstrates that the supreme ground of our faith is not argument or reasoning, but a personal encounter with Christ, whose living presence banishes our doubts. It is by drawing close to him that our faith grows and doubt is restrained.

So what happens in this encounter with Thomas? And how does it help us understand how we are to know Christ more fully and authentically? It is important to realise that the twentieth chapter of John relates two stories of encounters with Christ that banish doubt. The first is with Mary, in the aftermath of the resurrection. The disciples return to the tomb on the Sunday morning, and find it empty. They are devastated. Not only has their Lord been crucified, but someone has removed his body so they cannot even pay proper respect to his corpse. All except Mary leave the garden.

> Mary stood weeping outside the tomb. As she wept, she bent over to look into the tomb; and she saw two angels in white, sitting where the body of Jesus had been lying, one at the head and the other at the feet. They said to her, 'Woman, why are you weeping?' She said to them, 'They have taken away my Lord, and I do not know where they have laid him.' When she had said this, she turned round and saw Jesus standing there, but she did not know that it was Jesus. Jesus said to her, 'Woman, why are you weeping? For whom are you looking?' Supposing him to be the gardener, she said to him, 'Sir, if you have carried him away, tell me where you have laid him, and I will take him away.' Jesus said to her, 'Mary!' She turned and said to him in Hebrew, 'Rabbouni!' (which means Teacher).
>
> (John 20:11–16)

There is no attempt on the part of the risen Christ to persuade Mary with rational arguments that he is risen. Christ does not offer any logical proof of his resurrection. He simply speaks Mary's name, and she responds with his. *She recognises him*. That is all that is needed. Mary's fears, doubts and anxieties melt away. Having encountered and recognised Christ, she cannot doubt any longer.

In the case of Thomas, we find a more extended account of a series of specific doubts relating to the resurrection. It was too good to be true. Others were convinced of Christ's resurrection; Thomas was not.

But Thomas (who was called the Twin), one of the twelve, was not with them when Jesus came. So the other disciples told him, 'We have seen the Lord.' But he said to them, 'Unless I see the mark of the nails in his hands, and put my finger in the mark of the nails and my hand in his side, I will not believe.' A week later, his disciples were again in the house, and Thomas was with them. Although the doors were shut, Jesus came and stood among them and said, 'Peace be with you.' Then he said to Thomas, 'Put your finger here and see my hands. Reach out your hand, and put it in my side; do not doubt, but believe.' Thomas answered him, 'My Lord and my God!' Jesus said to him, 'Have you believed because you have seen me? Blessed are those who have not seen and yet have come to believe.'

(John 20:24–9)

Christ knows Thomas. He knows his weakness and his doubts, and is able to offer him the reassurance he needs. Thomas' response is one of the greatest confessions of the New Testament: 'My Lord and my God!'

If only we had been there to see it! If only we had been there to see any of the events on which our faith is grounded! We were not there to see Christ betrayed by the kiss of a friend, nor to see him cruelly nailed to the cross. Our ears were never privileged to hear the seven last words from the cross. We were not even there to see his broken and bruised body being taken down from the cross and lovingly placed in a borrowed tomb. Others had that privilege, but not us. We were not there when the risen Christ appeared to his disciples. Neither, as it happens, was Thomas. Yet we were not there to see Thomas' doubts resolved so gloriously. Had our eyes seen those wounds, or our fingers touched them, we too might have been able to cry in response 'My Lord and my God!' But we were not there.

Perhaps anticipating such thoughts, Christ speaks to us through this encounter, and we must listen closely to what is being said. 'Have you believed because you have seen me? Blessed are those who have not seen and yet have come to believe.' Thomas was able to present his doubts to the risen Christ, and found all his secret fears resolved. It was easy for him. Christ's words help us to see that the quality of our faith is greater still. Not having seen, we believe. We realise that Christ is all that we could ever hope to know and possess, and cling to him. Jesus encounters us as doubters – as a Thomas, who holds back, wanting reassurance, wanting proof, wanting certainty. In the end, we have to realise that we can never hope to finally eliminate our doubts and must throw ourselves into the waiting arms of the compassionate Christ. He will never let us go and never let us down.

Trusting God tends to be something we do on special occasions. Yet it ought to be our normal mode of living – a settled habit of trusting, nurtured by a constant closeness to God. I found this idea developed clearly in a work entitled *The Practice of the Presence of God* by Brother Lawrence of the Resurrection (1611–91). Lawrence tells of an insight he gained at the age of sixteen, which remained with him throughout his life. He found himself contemplating a tree in the depths of winter, stripped bare of its leaves. Yet he knew that, with the coming of spring, 'the leaves would be renewed, and after that the flowers and fruit appear'. It was not something he need worry about. He could trust that renewal would come in its own good time. In the same way, we should have a settled trust in God which sustains us in times of spiritual dryness. As Lawrence puts in, we should use both our minds and our imaginations to 'establish ourselves in the presence of God'.

This means learning to trust God at all times, and cultivating the practice of spending time in his presence in moments of quiet and repose rather than just in times of crisis. 'We need only to realise that God is close to us and to turn to him at every moment.' Trusting God is not a skill that we should suddenly need to acquire when in need; it is an attitude towards God

which we should practise until it becomes natural to live in this
way.

12

The failure: Peter

The Gospels portray Peter as the leader of the band of disciples who are called by Christ and leave all to follow him. Yet Peter is also depicted as a man with weaknesses, a man to whom we can easily relate. The encounters between Christ and Peter speak to us powerfully of the role of failure in the life of faith, and of our need to be recommissioned by Christ.

Perhaps the best place to begin this exploration is the tragic scene in the courtyard of the high priest in Jerusalem, in which Peter found all his illusions concerning himself being stripped away. Believing himself to be strong, he was exposed as weak. We can only guess at his sense of failure. So how did this situation develop? We may pick up the narrative in Mark's Gospel, as Christ and his disciples are walking towards the Mount of Olives after the Last Supper.

Jesus said to them, 'You will all become deserters; for it is written, "I will strike the shepherd, and the sheep will be scattered." But after I am raised up, I will go before you to Galilee.' Peter said to him, 'Even though all become deserters, I will not.' Jesus said to him, 'Truly I tell you, this day, this very night, before the cock crows twice, you will deny me three times.' But he said vehemently, 'Even though I must die with you, I will not deny you.'

(Mark 14:27–31)

It is easy to visualise this scene. Peter's commitment to Christ is total. He believes passionately that he will not abandon Christ, whatever pressures he will face. How could he ever do such a thing? Yet Christ knows Peter better than Peter knows himself. Never ceasing to love Peter, Christ gently chides him. Whatever Peter may think, he lacks the strength he will need in the tempestuous times that lie ahead.

Peter will not hear of this. He will *never* deny Christ. Yet within hours, the possibility that he could not contemplate came to pass. While warming himself by a fire after the arrest of Christ, Peter was confronted by a servant-girl, one of the least significant people in the household of the high priest. Despite all his boasting of bravery and commitment, Peter proves unable to cope with this very modest threat.

While Peter was below in the courtyard, one of the servant-girls of the high priest came by. When she saw Peter warming himself, she stared at him, and said, 'You also were with Jesus, the man from Nazareth.' But he denied it, saying, 'I do not know or understand what you are talking about.' And he went out into the forecourt. Then the cock crowed. And the servant-girl, on seeing him, began again to say to the bystanders, 'This man is one of them.' But again he denied it. And after a little while the bystanders again said to Peter, 'Certainly you are one of them; for you are a Galilean.' But he began to curse, and he swore an oath. 'I do not know this man you are talking about.' At that moment the cock crowed for the second time. Then Peter remembered that Jesus had said to him, 'Before the cock crows twice, you will deny me three times.' And he broke down and wept.

(Mark 14:66–72)

The pool of tears that Peter shed then has since welled into an ocean as others have realised how they have failed their Lord. How many have promised themselves and promised the Lord that they would never let him down? And how many, whether through weakness or downright rebelliousness, betray him? Tears give way to anxiety: will the one whom we so shamefully failed ever have us back? Is there any way back into the embrace of the one we so shamefully spurned when a lesser good came our way?

Yet such moments of failure can be redemptive. They speak to us of our weakness, pride and arrogance. They open our eyes to the personal demons which inhabit our worlds and shape our destinies. They suddenly bring into sharp focus the extent to which we trust in our own strength and wisdom. When we fail, our personal weakness and frailty is exposed – sometimes only to ourselves, but often in a more humiliating manner, to a greater audience.

Christ breaks the hard heart, and heals the broken one. There are times when we need to hear sweet and tender words of reassurance. There are other times, however, when we need to be broken. Christ takes no pleasure in breaking us, nor is his ultimate aim to leave us shattered. His goal in breaking us down is to put us back together in a renewed and more spiritual manner. The case of Peter helps us understand something of how Christ deals with us in this way.

For Peter's failure did not mark the end of his ministry; it made possible a new beginning. Christ recommissioned his failed yet willing servant, whose fault lay supremely in his failure to know his own weaknesses. The encounter with Christ which marks this transition to restoration takes place by Lake Galilee (otherwise known as 'the Sea of Tiberias', related in the final chapter of John's Gospel). It is impossible to read of this encounter without becoming aware of the deep symbolism which lies only just beneath the surface of the narrative (John 21:1–19).

The passage opens with Peter and others by the shore of Lake Galilee. In Christ's absence, they have drifted back to their former occupation. They are fishermen all over again – but not, as the narrative makes clear, especially successful fishermen. They have cast their nets all night and caught nothing. Then a strange figure arrives on the shoreline. Maybe they knew who it was from the moment he appeared. Maybe they dared not hope that they were right. The mysterious figure invites them to cast their net to the right-hand side of the boat – and suddenly it is full of fish. The incident immediately calls to mind the first calling of the disciples, as narrated in Luke's Gospel (Luke 5:2–10). It is as if history is repeating itself. The seven disciples present on this occasion are being called again. This time, it is the risen Lord who calls them.

Although there are seven disciples present at this encounter, it is clear that the encounter with Peter is of supreme importance. Christ meets with Peter by the shore of the lake, standing by a fire on which some fish are cooking, with some bread nearby. The fish and bread immediately recall the great miracle of the feeding of the five thousand, in which Christ's power over creation and his compassion for his people were publicly demonstrated. Peter could hardly have failed to miss this powerful echo of the past.

Yet we must not overlook the significance of the fire. The fire was associated with denial and failure. It was by a fire that Peter had denied Christ three times in the courtyard of the high priest. For each of Peter's denials, Christ now offers him the opportunity to undo the past and begin again. Three times – once for each denial – Christ asks Peter whether he loves him. Peter clearly finds this a painful experience, but affirms his love for Christ in the face of the persistent questioning. For each affirmation of Christ, Peter is offered a task – that of caring for the people of God. He is to feed Christ's sheep, and tend his flock. As if to bring home to Peter how costly this commission is going to be, Christ hints at the manner of Peter's death. But Peter is not going to fail Christ again. Knowing his own weakness, yet also taking strength from the personal presence of his risen Lord, he makes his vow: he will not let Christ down again.

I have constantly found this helpful in my own development. We need to be reminded both of our failures, on the one hand, and of the power and the presence of Christ to renew us, on the other. For Martin Luther, the Christian life was to be seen as a constant process of returning to the foot of the cross to confess our sins and begin all over again. We can see something of this in Peter's encounter with Christ. Peter made his peace with Christ by the shores of Galilee. There is much to be said for returning to the place at which our Christian life began when we are aware of our need for renewal and refreshment. Perhaps it was a church in which we first heard the good news, or a room in which someone spoke of knowing Christ. Special places have an important role to play in our journey of faith, and they must never be despised.

Peter's recommissioning takes place alongside a symbol of his personal failure: the fire reminded him of the moment when he let Christ down. It is helpful to have something to bring to mind moments when we have failed Christ. Perhaps it might be a photograph of a person we have let down, or a letter telling us of a serious situation which has arisen on account of some foolish behaviour on our part, or incautious words we spoke. The more we appreciate our failures, the more we will realise the immensity of Christ's graciousness in allowing and enabling us to begin again.

Yet alongside those dark symbols of past failure we must also place symbols of the power and presence of Christ. The fish and the bread would have reminded Peter of the past, calling to mind the faithfulness and power of his Lord. As we have seen, one of the keys to knowing Christ is remembering his past goodness. It helps to have physical reminders of that goodness – things that we can see and touch. For many Christians, the most powerful and poignant of such reminders are the bread and wine by which Christ himself commanded us to remember him.

The Gospels tell of other encounters between Christ and those in need. These encounters lead to judgement, healing, forgiveness or restoration. Many of them concern Christ during his earthly ministry; others concern his encounters as the risen Lord. The risen Christ who made himself known as he walked alongside the disciples on the road to Emmaus (Luke 24:13) encounters us today, knocking on the door of our life and asking to be known as he knows us. Christ is no mere concept; he is a living reality, who encounters us as he encountered Saul of Tarsus on the road to Damascus. The same Christ who met and transformed Saul meets us today, longing to transform us, remove the scales from our eyes and send us to the ends of his world as his emissaries and ambassadors. To know Christ through his encounters is to appreciate how he transfigures lives and changes futures. Let us pray that he will continue to encounter us in this same way.

PART 4

Knowing Christ through his images

The Bible is replete with images, designed to stimulate our God-given faculties to long to know more about our Saviour and the benefits which he brings. Christ may be known more fully by reflecting on these images and the insights which they bring us. It is therefore important to spend some considerable time meditating on such images, refusing to rush onwards to the next passage, but lingering in anticipation of the nourishment and wisdom which they will impart.

Appreciating a biblical image takes time. It requires us to create space for reflection and inner absorption. Both the imagination and the mind are called into play as we try to ascertain what we are meant to gain through the images of Christ so skilfully and compellingly deployed throughout the Gospels, and especially in the Gospel of John. Images should arrest us and detain us precisely because they compel us to pause and reflect on what they convey. It is not simply what is conveyed but the means by which this takes place which engages our attention. We brood over its substance as much as its form, and emerge from that rumination with a fresh vision of the truth which lies *behind* it as much as it lies *in* it.

Images *force* us to use our imaginations, and hence to unleash the power of this God–given faculty for reflection and discernment. To appreciate this point, imagine for a moment that you are watching one of Shakespeare's plays in a theatre, or perhaps on television. The actors' faces and costumes and the theatrical sets are all visible to you. You do not need to imagine what they are like, because they are presented to you. Now imagine that you are listening to that same drama being transmitted by a radio station, or that you have managed to obtain an audio recording of the play and are listening to it as you drive to work. This time there is no picture to see. The only medium being presented to you is sound. As a result, you have to *imagine* what the characters look like. You have to create in your mind an impression of what the settings look like. Instead of being presented with ready–made images, you are forced to generate your own. Many people actually prefer the medium of radio for this very reason.

The biblical witness to God is very like an audio tape of a drama or novel. You are given a picture of God in words, not a series of photographs. You must reflect upon the nature and character of God in terms of the verbal images which you are given. Each of these is capable of giving several invaluable insights into God, but demands that you think seriously and reflectively about the image. It is like cracking open the shell of a hard nut in order to extract the sweet kernel inside.

To open up the imaginative possibilities of such an engagement, we may spend a few moments exploring a familiar statement from the opening chapter of John's Gospel. When John the Baptist sees Christ coming towards him, he declares: 'Here is the Lamb of God who takes away the sin of the world!' (John 1:29). It is clear that John expects this image of the 'Lamb of God' to convey insights concerning the identity of Christ to those standing around. Like a seed, it is meant to fall into the fertile ground of a biblically nourished imagination and to burst into growth, yielding the fruit of a deepened appreciation of Christ.

So how does this image stimulate the praying imagination, to help us know Christ more fully? It opens up some highly productive lines of reflection, of which the following are typical:

1   The image of the 'Lamb of God' immediately calls to mind the great Passover celebrations of Israel, which recalled God's faithfulness in delivering his people from captivity in Egypt (Exodus 12). A Passover lamb would be slain, as a reminder of God's continuing care for his people and commitment to them in conditions of adversity and suffering. To think of Jesus as this lamb of God is to see him as linked with God's great actions of deliverance, including the liberation of his people from their bondage to sin and the fear of death.

2   Yet the image possesses still deeper associations. The prophecy of Isaiah speaks of a coming Suffering Servant, who will be slain, like a lamb, for his people (Isaiah 53). This suffering servant of God was 'wounded for our transgressions, crushed for our iniquities' (Isaiah 53:5). This prophecy of Christ compares him to 'a lamb that is led to the slaughter' (Isaiah 53:7), on whom the guilt and sin of the world is laid. Perhaps John the Baptist had this rich vein of biblical prophecy in mind when he spoke of Christ as 'the Lamb of God *who takes away the sin of the world*'. This immediately suggests an affinity with the scapegoat (Leviticus 16:21–2), which was sent into the wilderness bearing the sin of God's people.

3   The image also brings out poignantly the meekness of Christ. A lamb is an image of weakness and gentleness. Is not one of the greatest paradoxes of the Christian faith that the redemption of the world was brought about by what the world regarded as foolish and weak (1 Corinthians 1:18–25)? The book of Revelation celebrates the triumph of that lamb. The one who was slain in weakness is raised in glory, to the acclamation of the heavenly host: 'Worthy is the Lamb that was slaughtered, to receive power and wealth and

wisdom and might and honour and glory and blessing!'
(Revelation 5:12).

There is no doubt that this powerful image can spark off still
more lines of thought, encouraging the forging of important
biblical connections and the establishing of solid grounds for
Christian prayer and adoration. Yet our engagement with this
image was purely preliminary, in order to encourage us to
become more deeply engaged with the process of reflection on
other such images.

The four images that will form the basis of our reflection in
the remainder of this section are all drawn from John's Gospel. It
is clear that the writer of this Gospel has a deep appreciation of
the importance of visual images, or 'signs', and their ability to
convey theological and spiritual insights. John is himself quite
clear as to why he wrote his Gospel:

> Now Jesus did many other signs in the presence of his
> disciples, which are not written in this book. But these [that
> is, the ones that *are* included] are written so that you may
> come to believe that Jesus is the Messiah, the Son of God, and
> that through believing you may have life in his name.
>
> (John 20:30–1)

John's Gospel can be thought of as an extended presentation of
the identity and significance of Jesus, with the aim of leading its
readers to share the author's life-giving and life-changing faith.

John's Gospel is particularly noted for its seven 'I am' sayings,
which are found on the lips of Jesus in this Gospel alone. The
first of these sayings is found at John 6:35, in which Jesus speaks
the following words: 'I am the bread of life.' Each of the sayings
picks up some major themes from the Old Testament (such as
Israel as a vine, Moses as the giver of the bread from heaven, and
God as the shepherd of Israel), and applies them directly to Jesus.
The form of these sayings is grammatically unusual, making them

stand out from the remainder of the text. This point is probably a little difficult for readers not familiar with Greek to appreciate; however, the importance of the point is that there is a direct similarity between these sayings and Exodus 3:14, in which God reveals himself to Moses as 'I am who I am'. There thus seems to be an implicit declaration of divinity on the part of Jesus within each of these sayings. The seven 'I am' sayings can be set out as follows:

6:35	The bread of life
8:12, 9:5	The light of the world
10:7, 9	The gate for the sheep
10:11	The good shepherd
11:25	The resurrection and the life
14:6	The way, the truth and the life
15:1, 5	The true vine

Affirmation must generate meditation, as we ask what these images are meant to convey. How does meditating on Christ as 'the true vine' or the 'bread of life' help us to know him better?

The main point to notice is the form which these statements take. Christ is not represented as saying 'I show you the way' or 'I make it possible for you to have life', or even 'I teach you the truth'. The statements are emphatic: it is Christ himself who *is* the way, the truth and the life. He is not merely the agent through whom certain benefits are gained, wonderful though those benefits may be. The 'I am' sayings proclaim the utter inseparability of giver and gift, of person and benefit.

13

The bread of life

'I am the bread of life' (John 6:48). What does this image have to say to us? How does this striking statement illuminate the privileges to be gained through knowing Christ? Perhaps the best way of reaping the rich harvest of the image is to allow our minds to focus on its words and see how we find ourselves led.

Bread . . . the image instantly suggests the idea of being nourished, of meeting the specific human need of hunger. We are immediately reminded of our spiritual emptiness. We may find that we are satisfied physically, but a deeper hunger remains – a hunger for meaning, for immortality, for something that is profoundly satisfying. To speak of Christ as bread is to establish a connection with human hunger and emptiness. What humanity needs, Christ provides.

This line of thought is confirmed by the further development of this image in the passage. Jesus declares that he is the bread of life; 'whoever comes to me will never be hungry, and whoever believes in me will never be thirsty' (John 6:35). The themes of hunger and thirst are now brought together. Both point to human needs and affirm the ability of Christ to meet these. Note how the language of 'coming' and 'believing' is used in relation to Christ. The emptiness of the Christless human condition can be transformed by coming to him and believing in him.

To speak of Christ as 'bread' is to propose an analogy between the two. Now analogies are never identities, and we must always recall that an analogy points to similarities and dissimilarities. Christ is like bread in that he satisfies the hunger of the human heart. Yet everyone who eats bread will hunger again. It is at best a short-term fix, a temporary solution to a deep and radical problem. Is there anything that can satisfy us permanently?

We find this question anticipated in one of the most moving encounters of Jesus. In his conversation with the Samaritan woman, the themes of 'water' and 'thirst' become highly significant. The woman hopes to draw water from a well, and so to slake her own thirst and that of her people. Christ discerns a deeper thirst which water is incapable of satisfying. 'Everyone who drinks of this water will be thirsty again, but those who drink of the water that I will give them will never be thirsty. The water that I will give will become in them a spring of water gushing up to eternal life' (John 4:13–14). What Christ offered this woman – and what he continues to offer us to this day – is something more. Christ offers to create within us a permanent spring of living water which will perpetually quench our thirst. We need no longer look outside ourselves for spiritual resources; they will be provided from within, on account of the 'spring of water' within us.

Yet this 'spring of water' will do more than satisfy: it will lead to eternal life. At this point, we find the image of 'bread' being explored in a similar and highly important way:

I am the bread of life. Your ancestors ate the manna in the wilderness, and they died. This is the bread that comes down from heaven, so that one may eat of it and not die. I am the living bread that came down from heaven. Whoever eats of this bread will live for ever; and the bread that I will give for the life of the world is my flesh.

(John 6:48–51)

Christ here makes the telling point that all those who eat of any earthly bread – even the manna which God provided for the people of Israel during their wilderness wanderings – will die. Bread offers sustenance during life; it cannot offer hope beyond it. Bread sustains us physically; it cannot sustain us spiritually, or open up the possibility of a new existence beyond the realm of the physical. Yet the 'bread of life' is rather different. As the 'bread of life', Jesus offers the hope of eternal life to those who feed on him. To know Christ is to experience this hope as a present reality, knowing that it is grounded in the trustworthiness of God.

Note also that feeding is itself an image of 'knowing Christ', affirming our need to absorb and appropriate Christ as an internal reality rather than as a remote external figure. Some Roman writers suspected the early Christians of cannibalism on account of the way in which they spoke of 'feeding on Christ' or 'eating the body of Christ'. Yet the language here is that of bringing Christ into the closest of relationships with the believer. The intimacy of the relationship which Christ desires with his people is represented in the Lord's Supper, in which Christians eat bread and drink wine as a memorial of the suffering and death of Christ.

Yet that hope is purchased at a price. The Christ who makes this promise of eternal life is the same Christ whose body must be broken as the means to that end. The Lord's Supper is, in part, an act of purposeful remembrance, a deliberate calling to mind of the pain of Calvary as the price of the Christian life. There is a double action of humility and service on the part of Christ here: his coming into the world, and his giving himself for that world. Each is an act of service: first, by setting aside his glory, stepping out of a world in which pain and suffering were unknown into a world in which they were only too well known; second, by accepting that pain and suffering as a means of purging our sin and guilt, and allowing us to draw close to him so that we might feed on him and have the hope of eternal life.

There is also a clear connection between Christ as the 'bread of life' and the great theme of 'manna' in the Old Testament accounts of the exodus from Egypt. The Lord, having led his people from captivity in Egypt, sustained them during the long period of their wanderings in the wilderness with 'bread from heaven' (Psalm 78:24; Nehemiah 9:15). God's graciousness in providing the manna finds its fulfilment in Christ, with manna being seen as an anticipation or foreshadowing of Christ himself. The true bread from heaven was not the manna in the wilderness – itself a sign rather than the greater reality to which it pointed.

The parallels between manna and the 'bread of life' also establish the continuity between the life of faith under the old and new covenants. The same God who redeemed his people from their bondage in Egypt also redeemed them from bondage to sin and the fear of death. The manna which nourished Israel and reassured her of God's continuing presence and care in the wilderness points to the way in which Christ nourishes and reassures us in the life of faith. The manna kept Israel going while she journeyed in hope to the Promised Land; Christ will sustain us as we travel to the New Jerusalem, whose door he has flung open wide to welcome us.

Having explored the way in which images can help us grasp the immense richness of Christ, we now turn to consider another.

14

The light of the world

'I am the light of the world' (John 8:12). According to John's Gospel, Christ spoke these words at the Jewish Feast of the Tabernacles, a ceremony in which the symbolism of light played a major role. We see here a further statement of a theme which was introduced in the opening verses of John's Gospel – that the true light has come into the world, which is not able to overcome it (John 1:5). To conceive of Christ as the 'light of the world' offers us important windows of perception into his identity and significance, illuminating what it means to know him.

To appreciate the power of this image, we may ask what the world would be like in the absence of light. Musing on this interplay of darkness and light allows us to grasp something of the significance of Christ for his world and his people. Darkness evokes fear and anxiety, not least the threat of being lost and unable to find our way. It is no accident that the great Italian poet Dante Aligheri (1265–1321) opens his *Divine Comedy* with a description of becoming lost in a dark wood:

> In the midst of the journey of our life
> I found myself in a dark wood
> For the direct road had been lost.

For Dante, the dark wood was a symbol of the sinful world, in which it was easy to become lost or engulfed by forces which lead us away from God.

In the summer of 1973, two friends and I set out to cycle around France. We crossed from the southern English port of Southampton to Le Havre, and rode south to explore the Loire valley. After a month, we headed back to Le Havre. The final stage of our journey to the port took us through Normandy. The quickest way of getting to Le Havre was to follow a road that was clearly marked on our maps through some of the great forests that still remain in that part of France. We calculated that it would take us about two hours to get through, and entered the forest at about six o'clock on a glorious summer's evening. We would easily be able to catch the morning ferry back to England.

It didn't work out like that. The forest engulfed us within ten minutes. The road seemed quite clear to begin with. However, the leaves of the great trees created a dense canopy over our heads. It became dark far earlier than we had anticipated, simply because the light of the setting sun could not penetrate the depths of the forest. At some point we must have taken a wrong turning. The path which we were following petered out, and we realised that we were lost. There were no landmarks of any kind to help us work out where we were or which direction we should take to get back on course. The map showed a major road to our north, so we strained our ears, listening for the noise of traffic, hoping that this would help us find our way. But all that we could hear was the wind gently rustling the leaves of the trees far above us. There was nothing we could do other than bed down for the night and wait for the dawn. The rising of the sun would allow us to find a path, and give us a sense of direction. But that was at least six hours away.

We spent the night huddled in sleeping bags, close to our cycles and to each other. We were engulfed in darkness, and could hear noises which might well have been nothing more than forest animals foraging for food – or which might have been more sinister. None of us found it easy to sleep that night. It evoked childhood memories of reading fairy tales from the Brothers Grimm, recounting with a certain relish the horrible fate that awaited people who got lost in the great forests of southern Germany.

In that situation, we had no doubts as to the importance of light. If some local farmer had driven through on a tractor, its headlights would have allowed us to locate both the road it was using and the direction it was taking to get out of the forest. Yet we could see nothing. We were surrounded by trees, unable to discern the obstacles in our path. It would have been madness to have pressed on. All we could do was wait in hope for the dawn.

For writers in biblical times, the night was also a time of potential danger and uncertainty. We see this reflected most clearly in the Old Testament image of watchmen waiting patiently for the dawn. 'I wait for the LORD, my soul waits, and in his word I hope. My soul waits for the LORD more than those who watch for the morning' (Psalm 130:5–6). The night was seen as a time of potential danger, when watchmen had to be posted throughout the city of Jerusalem in order to warn of any threat to the city which developed under the cover of darkness. The arrival of the dawn was seen as marking the end of this sinister possibility.

Dawn thus came to be associated with hope, or with a sense of relief. The ending of the night was often seen as an image of the end of a period of despair or misery. To speak of Christ as the 'light of the world' is thus to imagine the breaking of dawn on a new day in the history of the world – a day in which the people who walked in darkness have seen a great light (Isaiah 9:2). The messianic hopes of Israel were often expressed in terms of the dawning of the day of the Lord. Thus Malachi – the final prophet of the Old Testament era – looks forward to a time when God will come to visit and redeem his people (Malachi 3:1–4; 4:1–2), when the 'sun of righteousness shall rise, with healing in its wings' (Malachi 4:2).

Reflecting on the image of Christ as the light of the world against this background immediately allows us to appreciate its power. Light is about hope. The forces of darkness, which so often seem to overwhelm us, will finally be scattered by the radiance of the light of the world. John's Gospel opens with a powerful statement of the ultimate triumph of the light of the world over the darkness which has enveloped and enfolded it. Just as the rising sun scatters the darkness and burns off the mists which cloud the surface of the earth, so the coming of Christ offers the hope of illumination and warmth. To know Christ is to rejoice in the hope that he brings to this dark world.

So what difference does this make to us? One leading theme of the New Testament is that we may in some way mirror the light of Christ. To know Christ is to reflect his glory to our darkened world. If we are to think of ourselves as the 'light of the world' (Matthew 5:14), it is because we somehow reflect '*the* light of the world' (John 8:12).

When I was trying to understand this point, I found it helpful to think of the relation between Christ and ourselves in terms of the relation of the sun to the moon. As a young boy, I had long been interested in amateur astronomy, and had built myself a small telescope in order to be able to observe the moon, planets and stars. I realised that the moon was actually a dead world, which illuminated the night sky because it reflected the light of the sun. Furthermore, the moon reflected only a tiny proportion of the sunlight which fell upon it. Yet, despite this, the moon was able to light up a landscape by night, allowing people to see their way home. Having no light, no source of power of its own, it can still cast light on the earth by reflecting the brilliance of the sun. Though we have no glory of our own worth talking about, we have the privilege of reflecting the glory of Christ to the world, so that the world might see and respond.

15

The good shepherd

'I am the good shepherd' (John 10:11, 14). The image of a shepherd is so familiar that we have perhaps become insensitive to its riches. One of the most familiar biblical verses is Psalm 23:1, which affirms that 'the LORD is my shepherd'. Many Christians ask for this Psalm to be said or sung at their funerals, as it speaks so powerfully of the continuing love and care of God for his people, even in life's most difficult moments. This image of God as a shepherd is encountered frequently in the Old Testament (e.g. Psalm 80:1; Isaiah 40:11; Ezekiel 34:12), and is taken up and developed in the New Testament to refer to Jesus as the 'good shepherd'. But what does this image tell us about Christ?

It is clear that one of the most familiar insights yielded by this image is that of the loving care of the shepherd for his sheep. The shepherd was committed to his flock of sheep on a full-time basis. The shepherd tended to be regarded as a social outcast in Israel; the enormous amount of time he was obliged to spend with his flock prevented him from taking part in normal social activities, including religious observances. The image of God as a shepherd thus conveys the idea of the total commitment of God to his people. This notion is developed very powerfully in the New Testament, especially in the Parable of the Lost Sheep (Luke 15:3–7). The shepherd actively seeks out the lost sheep in order to bring it home, rejoicing.

Thinking of the Lord as a shepherd immediately speaks to us of *guidance*. The shepherd knows where food and water are to be found, and guides his sheep to them. It is he who finds the green pastures and quiet waters (Psalm 23:2) for his sheep. I was brought up in the Irish countryside, and remember often seeing flocks of sheep wandering aimlessly around the countryside, giving every impression of being lost. Left to themselves, sheep have a habit of straying and wandering off into dangerous countryside, getting stranded on hillsides. It is the shepherd who keeps the sheep on safe ground and ensures that they have food and drink. To liken the Lord to a shepherd is to emphasise his constant presence with his people, and his gentle guidance as he tries to protect them from the dangers which life offers and to bring them to a place of plenty and safety. 'He will feed his flock like a shepherd; he will gather the lambs in his arms, and carry them in his bosom, and gently lead the mother sheep' (Isaiah 40:11).

The image of the Lord as a shepherd also tells us something about ourselves. The Lord is a shepherd, and we are sheep, incapable of looking after ourselves and continually going astray. Human sinfulness is often compared with running away from God, like a stray sheep. 'All we like sheep have gone astray; we have all turned to our own way' (Isaiah 53:6; cf. Psalm 119:176; 1 Peter 2:25). And just as the shepherd goes to look for his lost sheep, so God came to find us in our lostness and bring us home. Just as the sheep learn to rely upon the shepherd for their existence, so we have to learn to depend upon the Lord. We may like to think that we are capable of looking after ourselves, but realism demands that we recognise just how totally dependent upon God we are, from birth to death.

Given the limitations of our resources as frail and fallen human beings, it comes as no surprise to learn that our shepherd does rather more than just point his sheep in the right direction, leading to the 'green pastures and still waters'. *He takes us there*, carrying those who are too weak to make the journey unaided (Isaiah 40:11). The Christian faith is not about God telling us where to go and what to do if we want salvation, then leaving us to get on with it. No – it is about God graciously accompanying, supporting and sustaining us as he journeys with us and guides us. Similarly, Christ declares and affirms that he is 'the way, and the truth, and the life' (John 14:6). Rather than merely show us the way that leads to eternal life, he sets us on that path and journeys with us as we travel. The great theme of 'Emmanuel' – God is with us (Matthew 1:23) – resounds throughout the Christian life as we remember that God is with us, even in life's darkest moments, guiding us to our eternal rest.

The image of the shepherd carrying a tired sheep to the safety of the fold is one of the most poignant of all the biblical images, and reminds us of the loving care of the Lord for his people. Yet John's Gospel intensifies this image: Christ is not merely a shepherd; he is the '*good* shepherd'. What is meant by this development of the image?

Perhaps the best way of exploring the intensification of the image of the shepherd is to note how each of the two affirmations of the image are immediately followed by an explanation or comment, offering a modest exposition of the new ideas: 'I am the good shepherd. The good shepherd lays down his life for the sheep' (John 10:11); 'I am the good shepherd. I know my own and my own know me' (John 10:14).

In what follows, we shall explore each of these points and how it leads to a vigorous transformation of an already potent symbol of the loving care of God for his people.

First, we are reminded that Christ willingly laid down his life for his own. Such is his commitment to those he loves that he gives everything that he has in order that they might have eternal life. This is the hallmark of the *good* shepherd, as opposed to a hired hand who is paid to look after the sheep but who has no personal interest in their welfare. Because the sheep are *his*, he is deeply concerned for their well-being. Each sheep is to be seen as one for whom the good shepherd laid down his life, and is thus endowed with a dignity and purpose which far exceeds their lowly status in the eyes of the world.

Second, we learn that the good shepherd knows his own, as he is known by them. We are presented with the image of a mass of sheep; collectively they constitute a flock, individually they have their own specific existence and cluster of hopes and fears. One of the most challenging insights we are forced to recognise here is that Christ knows us individually. No matter how many may count themselves as privileged to know Christ, he still knows each one individually. Each of us is special in his sight.

The image thus illuminates both the identity of Christ, and our own situation as his people. To know Christ is to know more about ourselves. We cannot know ourselves truly or fully without knowing, and being known by, Christ.

16

The true vine

'I am the true vine' (John 15:1). The image of a vine had long been used to depict Israel. The Old Testament speaks of Israel as a vine which was planted in the Promised Land. It took root and spread out to fill the territory (Psalm 80:8–9). At other points, Israel is compared to a vineyard, planted by the Lord (Isaiah 5:1–7). The use of this image thus immediately evokes memories of the history of Israel as God's vine, and the implicit claim of Christ to be the fulfilment of that history.

Yet the importance of this image for the theme of 'knowing Christ' lies in its emphasis *upon the need to be attached to Christ*. The believer is the branch, and Christ is the stock of the vine. In order to grow and achieve their full potential as believers, Christians must remain firmly and closely attached to Christ. Just as the sap from the vine is essential if the branch is to flourish and bear fruit, so we must remain in the closest and most intimate relationship with Christ. Apart from him, we can do nothing (John 15:5).

If we are separated from him, we will be unable to sustain our Christian existence, and will wilt and finally die. If that happens, we become like a dead piece of wood, of no use to anyone. The best that can be done with it is to burn it. There is no hint of condemnation here, least of all any suggestion that a believer who loses spiritual intimacy with Christ is thrown into the fires of hell, as some might suppose. The point being made is crisp and decisive: to grow in Christ, we must remain in Christ.

Before we consider the importance of this theme of 'attachment to Christ' in more detail, we may note that the Bible often depicts the essence of sin in terms of one of its effects – separation from the presence of God. 'Your iniquities have been barriers between you and your God, and your sins have hidden his face from you' (Isaiah 59:2). The importance of this theme of 'separation from God' can easily be overlooked. To appreciate its importance to the image of Christ as the 'true vine', we may consider some biblical images which develop this theme of separation from God in a little more detail. What is especially important to note here is that the gospel offers to abolish such separation, whatever form it may take, and restore us to closeness with God.

1   *Alienation from God.* Paul reminds his readers that they were once 'without Christ, aliens from the commonwealth of Israel, and strangers to the covenants of promise, having no hope and without God in the world' (Ephesians 2:12). Sin can be thought of in terms of being at war with God (Ephesians 2:14–16). Yet that hostility can be overcome. Christ is our peace, in that he has broken down the hostility between ourselves and God. He has made it possible for us to be reconciled to God, so that our alienation is abolished (2 Corinthians 5:19). Through Christ, we have been restored to fellowship with God.

2   *Expulsion from paradise.* On account of sin, Adam and Eve were expelled from Eden (Genesis 3:24). There could be no return to Eden; the way was blocked by the cherubim and a flaming sword. These are powerful images of the separation between God and humanity. Sin is a barrier between ourselves and paradise and the God who created us to dwell

there. We have become 'strangers and aliens' (Ephesians 2:19), who wander over the face of the earth in lonely isolation. Yet, through faith, we enter into a community – the people of God. Through Christ we are now 'citizens with the saints and also members of the household of God' (Ephesians 2:19). Notice again how salvation is understood as being restored to fellowship with God. The barriers of separation have been overcome and removed. Heaven is to be seen as our final and permanent restoration to the presence of God, when those who were expelled from Eden are welcomed into the New Jerusalem.

An important related idea is that of *rejection*. The expulsion of Adam and Eve from Eden is an aspect of their rejection by God. On account of their sin, they are denied access to the presence of God and to the blessings which he had intended for them. Sin excludes us from the fellowship of God. This does not arise on account of some human inability to find God. It is a result of disobedience, a decision to reject God. In order for the situation to be changed and for fellowship to be restored, God must be able to accept those whom he has rejected. Once more, the importance of the theme of *reconciliation* will be obvious. Through the saving death of Christ on the cross, God accepts those who were once unacceptable, and brings close those who were far away.

3 *Going our own way.* 'All we, like sheep, have gone astray, we have all turned to our own way' (Isaiah 53:6). Choosing to go our own way inevitably means departing both from God's way and from God himself. Our desire for autonomy leads us to take paths of our own choosing which lead away from the God who created us. Perhaps one of the most memorable parables concerns a son who decides to go his own way (Luke 15:11–24). That resolution to 'go his own way' meant that the son chose to leave his father. Eventually, he deeply regretted his action and longed to be restored to his father's

presence. The story of the son's restoration to fellowship with his father is one of the most moving and powerful narratives in Scripture. The importance in this context will be clear – going our own way means going away from God, and becoming separated from him.

Biblical images of sin such as these lead us to an understanding that the core consequences of sin are separation from God at the *physical, personal,* and *moral* level. At the *physical level*, we are cut off from God on account of death, which is an integral aspect of sin. Through faith, we are assured of eternal life, in which we shall never again experience separation from God. 'For the wages of sin is death, but the free gift of God is eternal life in Christ Jesus our Lord' (Romans 6:23). At the *personal level*, our relationship of love and trust with God has been shattered. At the *moral level*, we are no longer in good standing with God. This is expressed in the Bible in terms of our unrighteousness in the light of God's holiness and justice. 'The LORD of hosts is exalted by justice, and the holy God shows himself holy by righteousness' (Isaiah 5:16). All of these are open to restoration on account of the salvation won by Christ on the cross.

Having noted the importance of 'separation' as a theme, let us now return to engage with the image of Christ as the 'true vine' in more detail. The basic theme is the absolute necessity to remain attached to Christ in order to live the Christian life. To become detached from him spells spiritual languishment and ultimately the loss of this life-giving relationship. 'Abide in me as I abide in you' (John 15:4). We are reminded here that the Christian life is grounded upon, sustained by and totally dependent upon a two-way relationship with the living Christ.

It is not enough to maintain the externals of faith. Some faithfully attend church, yet find it devoid of any meaning. Some obediently believe in the truth of the Christian creeds, yet find that these make no difference to their lives whatsoever. Others repeat the Christian vocabulary they learned as children, knowing in their heart of hearts that it has ceased to have any real connection with their lives. A living relationship with Christ is the difference between a faith which will grow and a faith which will die through lack of nourishment.

Notice also how remaining attached to Christ is the essential precondition to being useful for Christ. The branch will only bear fruit while it remains attached to the vine. If we want to serve Christ, we must know Christ. Spiritual intimacy is not an optional extra, something that we can do without while other acts of service for Christ take priority. Nurturing our personal relationship with Christ is essential if we are to do *anything* for him.

At times, I have been aware that the intimacy of my relationship with Christ has been seriously compromised, not least through overwork and distraction. The Parable of the Sower (Mark 4:3–9) makes the point that the seed of the gospel can easily be choked by the cares of the world. It is essential that we clear the ground for the seed of the gospel in our lives, making sure that nothing is allowed to overshadow, eclipse or compete with the growth of our faith.

Martin Luther made this point forcefully in his *Greater Catechism* (1529). Commenting on the first commandment, Luther offers us a way of checking on our spiritual vitality.

'You shall have no other God.' That is, you shall have me alone for your God. So what is said here, and what is its meaning? Answer: A god means that from whom we are to expect all that is good, and to whom we are to take refuge in every need. To have a God is therefore nothing else than to trust and believe in him with your entire heart. I have often said that the trust and faith of the heart alone can make both God and an idol. If your faith and trust are right, then your god is also right. On the other hand, if your trust is false and wrong, then you do not have the true God; for these two belong together – faith and God. So I say that, *whatever your heart depends upon, and wherever your heart is fixed — that is actually your god.*[15]

Luther's words are a powerful challenge to examine ourselves, and determine whether we have accidentally allowed something or someone else to become god to us. I have often found it helpful to keep a checklist and note the things that seem to be top of my list of priorities at any one time. Perhaps it will come as little surprise to learn that my thoughts constantly wander away from Christ to more mundane matters; they may seem more important at the time, but in reality are not that significant.

We must never allow anything that is less than Christ to take the place of Christ himself. Other things will pass away and lose their lustre. He remains. We find this thought superbly expressed in a hymn of Bernard of Clairvaux (1090–1153):

> Jesus, Thou Joy of loving hearts,
> Thou Fount of life, Thou Light of men,
> From the best bliss that earth imparts,
> We turn unfilled to Thee again.[16]

And by turning back to him from all the distractions of the world, we can ensure that our close and intimate relationship is resumed, in order that we may serve him afresh.

PART 5

Knowing Christ through his benefits

'To know Christ is to know his benefits' (Philip Melanchthon). I first read those words in 1977, when I was studying theology at Oxford University. They expressed succinctly a general principle that I had been feeling my way towards for some time. *To know Christ was to know what he had achieved for us.* To know the giver is to know the gifts. The generosity and character of the one who gives can be known more fully by reflecting on what we are given.

This seemed to me to open up a very helpful and illuminating way of thinking about how we know Christ, and to offer helpful possibilities of knowing him more intimately. It forces us to ask two penetrating questions:

- What did Christ achieve for us?
- Do we know these benefits as realities in our lives?

Perhaps one of the best ways of beginning this process of reflection is to reflect on the costliness of the benefits which Christ won for us.

17

The costliness of the benefits of Christ

Christ laid aside his majesty and glory in order to enter into this world to redeem us. Paul's famous 'hymn to Christ' (Philippians 2:5–11) sets this out with especial clarity. Christ chose to set aside his majesty and status in order to save us. We must appreciate what Christ gave up for us if we are to fully grasp the wonder of his love for us. He chose to humble himself and enter into this world as a slave, rather than as its rightful master and Lord. He who was rich beyond all splendour became poor for our sake. As Charles Wesley's famous hymn 'And can it be?' puts it:

> He left his father's throne above,
> So free, so infinite his grace.
> Emptied himself of all but love,
> And bled for Adam's helpless race.[17]

Christ was entitled to honour and glory; he chose to set it on one side in order to become our servant. We must never think of this in terms of Christ putting up with something undignified, or making the best of a bad situation. Christ insisted that servanthood was to be seen as the highest of callings, and demonstrated this by taking on this status himself. Incarnation is about both the affirmation and the embodiment of the values of the kingdom of God in Christ. When some of Christ's disciples fought over who would have the privilege of sitting at his right hand in the kingdom, Christ rebuked them by insisting that servanthood was the supreme privilege (Mark 10:44–5). By washing his disciples' feet shortly before his betrayal (John 13), Christ demonstrated the new status he had assigned to servanthood.

By becoming a slave, Christ affirmed the royal role of servanthood within the Christian community, and also manifested his commitment to believers. The full wonder of the extent to which God values us can only be appreciated when we recognise what the incarnation and crucifixion really mean. God humbles himself and stoops down to meet us where we are. Paul asks his readers to model that same humility in their dealings with each other.

So the Lord became a slave for us. This insight holds the key to a Christian understanding of humility. Christ stooped down to meet us, gladly lowering himself to where we are, so that he might raise us to where he is. It is only by reflecting on the full extent of Christ's humility – his entering into this world as a slave, suffering rejection and dying, spurned, on a cross – that we can even begin to grasp how much he loves us and wants us to be with him.

Martin Luther tried to capture something of the panorama of costly redemption in his *Greater Catechism* (1529), setting out the implications of following the Creed in believing 'in the Lord Jesus Christ':

But all the points which follow in order in this article serve no other purpose than to explain and express this redemption, how and whereby it was accomplished, that is, how much it cost Christ, and what he spent and risked in order that he might win us and bring us under his dominion, namely, that he became a human being, was conceived and born without sin of the Holy Ghost and of the Virgin Mary, that he might overcome sin; moreover, that he suffered, died and was buried, so that he might make satisfaction for me and pay what I owe, not with silver nor gold, but with his own precious blood. And all this, in order to become my Lord; for he did none of these for himself, nor had he any need for it.[18]

Luther here makes the point that Christ undertook all of this *for us*. He did not need to do this for himself, but chose to undertake it for each of us. There are two sides to this spiritual coin: appreciating on the one hand how precious Christ's death is to the believer; and, on the other, how precious we are to the Christ who died for us.

Christian reflection on the costliness of redemption has rightly focused on the cross. Christ died so that we might live. This terse statement sums up so much of the gospel message, and can act as a powerful reminder of the price of our redemption. I have often found it helpful to picture the scene of the crucifixion and hear the taunts of the mob around Christ, mocking him. One has always stood out for me: 'Save yourself! If you are the Son of God, come down from the cross' (Matthew 27:40). Yet precisely because he *was* the Son of God, he stayed there, obedient to the end.

But the vague reference to Christ 'dying' cannot be allowed to pass unchallenged. Christ did not merely die; he was *put to death* in one of the most grimly sadistic ways conceivable. The costliness of Christ's benefits must be framed by the harsh realities of the crucifixion.

Crucifixion was probably introduced as a form of capital punishment by the Phoenicians and Persians. The person to be executed would be raised up on a pole or some other kind of frame, partly as a means of killing the condemned person, and partly as a means of ensuring that his agony and fate were visible to as many as possible. The Romans made widespread use of crucifixion, seeing it as especially effective in discouraging rebellion within their far-flung empire. It was used ruthlessly to suppress rebellions in the provinces, including the revolt of the Cantabrians in northern Spain as well as those of the Jews. Josephus' accounts of the crucifixion of Jewish fugitives who attempted to escape from besieged Jerusalem at the time of its final destruction by Roman armies make horrifying reading.

In the view of most Roman jurists, notorious criminals should be crucified on the exact location of their crime, so that 'the sight may deter others from such crimes'. Perhaps for this reason, the Roman emperor Quintillian crucified criminals on the busiest thoroughfares, in order that the maximum deterrent effect might be achieved. Apart from traitors, crucifixion was usually reserved for slaves, military deserters and criminals from the lowest level of society. It created a deadly amalgam of sustained physical pain and social stigma. The executed person would be reviled.

For a Jew, however, crucifixion represented rather more than a particularly horrible mode of death. According to the Law, anyone hanged upon a tree was to be regarded as cursed by God (Deuteronomy 21:23), which would hardly commend the Christian claim that Jesus was indeed the long-awaited Messiah. Indeed, one of the Dead Sea scrolls suggests that crucifixion was regarded as the proper form of execution for a Jew suspected of high treason.

Crucifixion thus ensured that the person would be treated with revulsion by many of those who otherwise might have been sympathetic to him. An anti-Christian graffito, preserved from ancient Rome, depicts a man adoring a crucified man with the head of an ass. The inscription reads: 'Alexander worships his god.'

Since crucifixion was regarded with disgust by polite Roman society, hardly any detailed descriptions of how the process took place have been passed down to us. However, there is some important archaeological evidence available, including the skeletal remains of a crucified person found near Jerusalem.

Enough is generally known about Roman approaches to execution to allow us to reconstruct what happened on the hill outside Jerusalem called the 'place of the skull'. Three types of cross were in general use.

1   A simple pole in the ground (*crux simplex*), on which the victim was impaled. This does not correspond with the Gospel accounts of the crucifixion of Christ.

2   A T-shaped cross (*crux commissa*), in which the vertical piece of wood is joined directly to a cross-bar. The victim's arms would have been nailed or tied to the crossbar.

3   The Latin cross (*crux immissa*), in which the crossbar was attached to the vertical piece of wood slightly below its top. As a result, the vertical piece projected above the crossbar, and hence the head of the victim. This is widely agreed to be the type of cross used to crucify Christ, and accounts for the Gospel references to an inscription being placed above his head (Matthew 27:37).

There are reasons for supposing that the vertical pieces of wood were permanently fixed in the ground, and that the victim was forced to carry the crossbar from the place at which the sentence of death was pronounced to the place of execution outside the city. The condemned would have been accompanied by a small group of soldiers, who were responsible for attaching the victim's arms to the crossbar with nails or ropes, and raising the victim on the cross.

Some crosses were equipped with a *sedile* – a sort of small seat or peg, about halfway up the main beam of the cross. This served a double purpose. Not only did it stop the condemned man from falling off; it prolonged his agony. Crucifixion usually killed by making it increasingly difficult and painful to breathe. At times, death was hastened by the executioners, who would break the legs of their victims. This placed intense pressure on the victim's lungs, which could no longer function, and death usually followed swiftly. A final thrust from a spear or sword ensured that the victim was really dead. In various parts of the world, the Romans would leave the bodies of those who were crucified attached to the cross, both as a warning to others and as a means of adding to the disgrace and shame of the process of execution. Often these bodies would end up being eaten by wild dogs or lying unburied by the foot of the cross.

I found it – and still find it – helpful to mark the three hours which Christ spent on the cross by going to a church service. The 'Three Hours of the Cross' often take the form of an extended meditation on the 'Seven Last Words from the Cross', with periods of silence, prayer or hymn-singing. Others find it helpful to read one of the passion narratives from the Gospels, and try to imagine the pain and humiliation experienced by our Saviour during the three hours of the cross. The Passions of J. S. Bach have their origins in this context, and many find it moving to listen to the words and music, allowing them to recreate the Calvary scenario.

The seven last words from the cross

'Father, forgive them for they do not know what they are doing' (Luke 23:34).

'Truly I tell you, today you will be with me in Paradise' (Luke 23:43).

'Woman, here is your son . . . here is your mother' (John 19:26–7).

'My God, my God, why have you forsaken me?' (Matthew 27:46).

'I am thirsty' (John 19:28).

'It is finished!' (John 19:30).

'Father, into your hands I commend my spirit' (Luke 23:46).

At times, I am tempted to think that three hours is just too much time to spend doing this kind of thing. Yet I need to rebuke myself at this point. Our salvation is so precious a thing that we must never take it for granted or forget how much it cost. One of the reasons that so many Christians seem to take the price of their salvation so lightly is that they don't give it enough thought, or allow their imaginations to grasp the bleakness of that pathetic scene. All that I am being asked to do is spend three hours *thinking* about Calvary. Christ spent those three hours *suffering* on the cross. Surely this puts things in perspective?

Some of the hymns which are sung around Good Friday are remarkably useful in crystallising our appreciation of the costliness of the benefits Christ won for us. An excellent example is provided by an anonymous medieval Latin poem, sometimes attributed to Bernard of Clairvaux. I continue to find this a superb framework for reflecting on the pain of the passion.

> O sacred Head, sore wounded,
> with grief and shame weighed down,
> now scornfully surrounded
> with thorns, thine only crown:
> how pale thou art with anguish,
> with sore abuse and scorn!
> How does that visage languish
> which once was bright as morn!
>
> What thou, my Lord, has suffered
> was all for sinners' gain;
> mine, mine was the transgression,
> but thine the deadly pain.
> Lo, here I fall, my Saviour!
> 'Tis I deserve thy place;
> look on me with thy favour,
> vouchsafe to me thy grace.

What language shall I borrow
to thank thee, dearest friend,
for this thy dying sorrow,
thy pity without end?
O make me thine forever;
and should I fainting be,
Lord, let me never, never
outlive my love for thee.

Be near me when I'm dying
O show thy cross to me;
And to my succour flying
Come, Lord, and set me free.
These eyes, new faith receiving,
From Jesus shall not move;
For he who dies believing,
Dies safely through thy love.[19]

Read this poem slowly, lingering over its words while absorbing its meaning. Use your mind, heart and imagination to interact with each verse and extract its spiritual meaning. In what follows, I will simply note in the briefest of manners some of the things that impressed me; let me invite you to draw up your own list.

- As I use my *mind*, I begin to understand some of the key theological ideas. I should have been there on the cross; Christ was there, in my place, bearing the pain which should have been mine.
- As I use my *imagination*, I can see Christ on the cross, replete with crown of thorns, suffering great pain. I begin to gain a better appreciation of how precious a thing redemption is.
- As I allow this hymn to impact upon my *heart*, I am overwhelmed by the immensity of the love that the suffering Christ shows in dying for me. I know that I ought to respond in kind.

The hymn also begins to explore some of the benefits which Christ won for us on the cross. In view of the importance of this matter, we shall move on directly to establish the identity of some of these benefits.

18

Identifying the benefits
of Christ

One of the great tasks of theology is to unpack the riches of the Christian proclamation. At its best, theology is like holding a jewel up to the light and being exhilarated by the beauty of the facets that are reflected. It is like opening a dust-encrusted treasure chest and lifting out its precious contents, appreciating the brilliance of each individual item. Theology aims to set out the full richness of the Christian gospel for public inspection.

An analogy which I have found especially helpful in understanding the role of theology is that of a glass prism breaking up a beam of white light into the colours of the rainbow – red, orange, yellow, green, blue, indigo and violet. (The same physical principle lies behind a rainbow being produced when raindrops refract the light of the sun.) All that the prism does is to separate out these colours; they are already present in the beam of white light, but cannot be individually distinguished until the light is passed through the prism. Theology takes the Christian proclamation of Jesus Christ as Saviour and Lord, and identifies the individual themes, ideas and possibilities which are mingled together within this glorious amalgam.

It is this process of analysis or reflection which allows us to identify the benefits of Christ. The New Testament contains some scintillating themes and life-changing possibilities, all brought into being through the life, death and resurrection of Christ. To appreciate Christ fully, it is essential to grasp these themes and possibilities. Who Christ is can be disclosed through what Christ makes possible. So what does he make possible?

It is impossible to do justice to the 'boundless riches of Christ' in this section. We shall explore only a few themes, to illustrate both the richness of the Christian gospel at this point and the immense value of studying that gospel carefully, identifying and appreciating its individual components.

Adoption

Paul assures us that, through Christ, we have been adopted as the children of God (Romans 8:23; Galatians 4:5). This image, drawn from Roman family law, is seen by Paul as casting light on the privileges and place of Christians in their relationship with God. It is an image that demands to be understood in our minds, and appreciated in our hearts.

Adoption is relatively easy to understand. A family decides to grant a child who was not born within its bounds the same legal privileges as those children who were born within it. The adopted children will thus have the same inheritance rights as the natural children. Christians may therefore think of themselves as having been brought within the family of God and granted the same legal privileges as any natural children. And who is the natural child of God? None other than Christ himself. Paul thus makes the powerful point that all that God bestowed upon Christ as his Son will eventually be granted to us, as the children of God: 'We are children of God, and if children, then heirs, heirs of God and joint heirs with Christ – if, in fact, we suffer with him so that we may also be glorified with him' (Romans 8:16–17).

The family marks of the children of God are thus suffering in this life and the promise of glory in the life to come. Glory lies beyond suffering, and we must learn to see suffering as a privilege to be borne gladly as a consequence of our new status.

Notice how the image of adoption highlights the importance of the theme of knowing Christ. Christ is the public manifestation of the destiny of believers. What God granted to him will also be granted to us. We are called to reflect upon Christ as the ground, guarantor and goal of the Christian life. Each of these deserves further comment.

1 Christ is the *ground* of our redemption, in that his death and resurrection throw open the door which leads to eternal life and salvation. These benefits can be obtained in no other way and by no other person. Meditating on the cross, as we have seen, is one of the ways of appreciating the costliness of the privileges we have been granted through Christ.

2 Christ is the *guarantor* of our redemption, in that his death and resurrection demonstrate the total reliability of the God who promises to see us through from death to eternal life. Reflecting on what God bestowed upon Christ reassures us that those same benefits and privileges will be bestowed upon his adopted, as well as natural, children.

3 Christ is also the final *goal* of our journey of faith. Where Christ has gone, we shall follow. He has been glorified, and we gladly and patiently await the promise of being clothed in his glory. This is why Paul urges his readers to raise their eyes heavenward (Colossians 3:1–3), in order that they may regain a sense of wonder and anticipation of finally arriving at journey's end, where Christ awaits us with open arms.

Yet the image of adoption appeals to our imaginations and hearts, not just to our minds. It cries out to be imaginatively rendered, not just understood. For adoption is about *being wanted*. It is about *belonging*. These are deeply emotive themes, which resonate with the cares and concerns of many in our increasingly fractured society. To be adopted is to be invited into a loving and caring environment. It is to be welcomed, wanted and valued. Adoption celebrates the privilege of invitation, in which the outsider is welcomed into the fold of faith and love.

Eternal life

One of the most compelling themes of the gospel is the challenge it poses to death. Death is robbed of its power to terrify and to separate us from those whom we love. The New Testament sets out this vision of the defeat of death and the enabling of a new way of life, liberated from the fear of death, in terms of two themes: the resurrection from the dead, and eternal life. It is the second of these that we shall consider in what follows.

The theme of eternal life plays a major role in the New Testament. 'For the wages of sin is death, but the free gift of God is eternal life in Christ Jesus our Lord' (Romans 6:23). The meaning of the phrase 'eternal life' is not immediately obvious. At first sight, it might seem to mean something like 'the same old life that we're used to, except extended infinitely'. That's not necessarily good news. It is certainly not good news for slaves, oppressed people and those suffering from pain through chronic illness.

Yet this rests on a misunderstanding of both the words 'eternal' and 'life'. 'Eternal life' does not mean an infinite extension of the pain, exhaustion, sorrow and suffering of the present life. It designates a new quality of life, a new way of being, in which the limitations of our old way of being are thrown off and we finally become what God would have us be. The Greek language has two words for life: *bios* and *zoe*. The first could be translated as something like 'biological existence', the process of getting by from one day to the next. The second means something rather more exciting and wonderful, designating life in all its fulness, a life really worth having. Eternal life is about life in all that fulness, which Christ bestows upon us and which nobody can ever take away from us. It is something which begins now, in a small yet real way, but which reaches its full wonder in the New Jerusalem.

19

Appropriating the benefits of Christ

Identifying the benefits which Christ offers us is one thing; accepting them is another. One of the great themes of Christian spirituality is the demand that we appropriate what is being offered us – that is, that we ensure that Christ is a present living reality within us, not an external guide and teacher who commands and guides us from a distance.

The New Testament uses a number of images to stress the importance of being connected up with Christ, and allowing him to participate in the dynamics of our personal existence.

Jesus is the bread of life, on whom we must feed if we are to benefit from his person and work (John 6:50–1). Bread which is not eaten cannot benefit or transform us. The image of eating is a compellingly significant means of bringing home to us the need to absorb Christ into the fabric of our being, to assimilate him into our lives, not simply as participant but as lifegiver and Lord.

Jesus is the one who reconciles us to God (2 Corinthians 5:18–19). The offer of reconciliation is real. Yet for it to transform our existence, it is something that must be accepted. Reconciliation is a two-way street, which both persons need to accept and internalise if the relationship is to be renewed and transformed.

The initiative has already been taken, in that Christ has entered into this world to show the extent to which we have become alienated from God, to demonstrate beyond doubt the love of God for us, and to invite us to restoration and renewal.

Perhaps the need to internalise the person and the benefits of Christ can best be grasped by developing one of the most telling images of Christ and his gospel – our need for healing. Christ declared that those who were ill needed the help of a doctor (Mark 2:17). What insights does this offer us? Perhaps the best way of exploring this issue is to turn to a story from the history of medicine.

On 3 September 1928, Alexander Fleming (1881–1955) returned to his laboratory at St Mary's Hospital, Paddington, London, from his summer vacation. He had been invited to contribute a section to a major forthcoming work, *A System of Bacteriology*. Fleming had been asked to write on staphylococci, spherical bacteria which were known to be responsible for many infections within the human body. In particular, they were responsible for turning wounds septic, and had led to countless deaths in World War I. Fleming had spent the previous few months cultivating these bacteria in special shallow circular glass containers, usually known as 'Petri dishes'. A small amount of nutrient gel ('agar') was added to these Petri dishes, after which bacteria were introduced to the culture and allowed to grow. The dishes were maintained at the temperature of the human body to simulate the conditions under which they would reproduce in a genuine infection.

By the end of July 1928, Fleming had finished his investigations, and he went on holiday for the month of August. Always an untidy man, he appears to have decided to clean up his laboratory on his return. As a result, Petri dishes with live bacteria cultures were left around on working surfaces in the laboratory. Two accidents then intervened. First, another research group, working in the same building as Fleming, had been experimenting on moulds found in the houses of people suffering from asthma. C. J. La Touche had been investigating a theory that asthma was triggered by certain moulds which infested the basements of the cold and damp houses of the period, and had gathered samples of such moulds. One of these appears to have been the mould *penicillium notatum*, a rare mould which – and here is the point of this digression – produces exceptionally large amounts of what we now know as penicillin. The mould had found its way into Fleming's laboratory, directly above La Touche's.

But this mould only produces penicillin at low temperatures. And here the second accident of history played its part. The weather patterns of British summers are notoriously unpredictable. As it happened, the first nine days of Fleming's summer vacation saw temperatures plummet in London. The laboratory became cold, and the mould produced far more penicillin than it would have under normal circumstances. It was enough to kill off the staphylococci around it.

Fleming returned from his summer holiday on 3 September and began to tidy up the laboratory. He took the Petri dishes containing bacterially infected agar and put them into a container full of Lysol, a powerful antiseptic. As he was doing this, he was interrupted by a visitor to the laboratory. D. M. Price, who had worked for Fleming in the past, had dropped by to see his former colleague. Fleming apologised for being so busy disinfecting Petri dishes, and lifted one up to show Price. He stared at it for a moment. 'That's funny,' he said.

What Fleming had seen was the Petri dish infected with the *penicillium* mould. He had noticed that the bacteria colonies close to the patch of mould on the dish had died, whereas those further away were unaffected. Fleming and his colleagues initially identified the mould as *penicillium rubrum*, but later realised it was the much rarer *penicillium notatum*. It was clear that this mould was producing some substance capable of killing bacteria. Fleming accordingly named this substance 'penicillin', but made no attempt to isolate the active chemical from the mould. He believed that penicillin would only be useful as an antiseptic for surface infections, and failed to appreciate that it could act as a powerful antibiotic for the general infections which had caused such huge death tolls during the war.

The story does not end there. As we have seen, Fleming did not really know what to do with his discovery. It was only through the later work of Howard Florey (1898–1968) and Ernst Chain (1906–79) at Oxford that the full potential of penicillin as an antibiotic was realised and ways of producing it in large quantities developed. By 1942, the antibiotic had been clinically tested and was ready for mass production. It was available in sufficient quantities to make a significant difference to the recovery rate of wounded service personnel in the Second World War. Fleming, Florey and Chain shared the Nobel Prize for Medicine in 1945 in recognition of their discovery. It is widely agreed that the discovery of penicillin saved more lives than any other discovery of the twentieth century.

The story is well known. So why tell it here? What place has it in a book on Christian spirituality? There are two points of no small importance which this critical episode illustrates, and which must be grasped if the full significance of knowing Christ is to be realised.

First, call to mind Fleming's Petri dish of the summer of 1928. The *penicillium* mould destroyed the colonies of bacteria close to it; those further away were unaffected. It was by coming into contact with the bacteria that the mould was able to exercise its healing potential. This has long been a major theme of Christian theology. Christ, with the power to save, must enter into the sinful human situation in order to change it. Why did God become incarnate? As we have seen, part of that answer is to demonstrate his total commitment to us and the immensity of his love for us. Yet there is another reason which we must note here. The incarnation is central to the process of healing and renewal of our fallen human natures.

We need to reflect on the Gospel passages which speak of people touching Christ, knowing that he has the power to heal them. Luke tells us of how crowds surged around Christ during his ministry; they knew that he could and would heal them. 'And all in the crowd were trying to touch him, for power came out from him and healed all of them' (Luke 6:19). Mark tells us of the woman with a haemorrhage, who knew that her only hope of being cured was to touch Christ the healer (Mark 5:25–34). So it is in the incarnation. By taking human nature upon himself, Christ was able to touch it and heal it. What needed to be healed was brought into the presence of the only one who could heal it. The fourth-century writer Gregory of Nazianzus put it like this: 'What has not been assumed has not been healed; it is what is united to his divinity that is saved.'

A second point must also be made. Penicillin serves no useful purpose if stored in a bottle in a laboratory. It needs to be *applied* if it is going to make a difference. Penicillin is now generally administered orally, in the form of tablets or a liquid suspension. Until and unless the antibiotic enters the human bloodstream and is conveyed to sites of infection through its circulation, it cannot destroy the bacteria which cause these potentially fatal infections. The antibiotic must be assimilated if it is to transform; it must be appropriated if it is to heal.

The importance of this theme for the Christian faith cannot be overstated. Christ does not heal us by external example, but by internal transformation. His power to save does not lie in his ability to tell us what God is like, but in his ability to become a living personal presence within our lives. The bread of life must be eaten; the water which springs up to eternal life must be drunk; the healing balm of the gospel must be applied. The old Negro spiritual got this exactly right:

> There is a balm in Gilead
> To make the wounded whole;
> There is a balm in Gilead
> To heal the sin-sick soul.

Yet this balm must be applied to the wounded soul if it is to be healed. We need to take it, apply it, make it our own, and allow it to do its God-given and God-empowered work.

When I was young, I developed a serious infection which had to be treated with antibiotics. I took my penicillin as directed by my doctor, and the infection quickly cleared up. Now I need to make it clear that I had not the slightest idea what the drug was, or how it worked. I just trusted the doctor's diagnosis and the cure that he prescribed. Many years later, as an Oxford undergraduate studying biochemistry, I learned how penicillin actually worked. As part of a course of lectures on the effects of drugs on living organisms, we were told about the way in which this antibiotic destroyed bacteria. Yet, I remember thinking at the time, it had worked perfectly well for me several years earlier, even though I didn't understand exactly what it did or how it did it.

There is a clear parallel here with the gospel proclamation of salvation in Christ, which diagnoses our problem (sin), and offers us a cure (Christ). It does not matter if we are unable to give a precise explanation of the mechanics of salvation. Theologians love to fuss over the details, and generally end up having ferocious arguments about things which do not always seem to be of great importance. The absolutely crucial thing is that Christ provides a solution to the problem of the human situation, and that we know how to benefit from that solution. And how do we do that? By appropriating both the benefits and the person of Christ. Or, to use the powerful language and imagery of St Patrick, the patron saint of my native Ireland, by 'binding' every aspect of the ministry of Christ to ourselves – that is, clasping it so that we never let go of it, and making it part of our lives and being.

It is perhaps easy to use our minds to grasp the importance of the points just being made. But our imaginations possess a capacity to make the point even more powerfully. Join me in creating a scenario in the theatre of your mind and entering into the experience of this world . . .

- You are in the company of the person who means more to you than anyone else, humanly speaking. You know that if they were taken away from you, life would be unbearable. Picture that person now.
- The two of you decide that you would like to go walking in the jungles of South America. The guide books you read speak of the immense and awesome vistas that you will encounter. You begin to anticipate the wonders that you will see. Perhaps you don't pay enough attention to the sections of those same guidebooks which warn of health risks and the difficulties of getting medical attention in remote areas.
- To get into the jungle, you decide to rent a car. Some of the areas the guide books recommend are not easily accessible by public transport. Hiring a car is clearly the easiest way of getting around.
- You crash the car, causing a serious wound in your companion's thigh. Fortunately, no major blood vessel is severed. You do what you can to patch up the damage. Your companion lies by the side of the road as you try to administer first aid. But the wound remains open. You notice that some soil has got into the wound.
- The wound becomes increasingly painful, and begins to swell. You notice signs of high fever, reddish-brown pus, and gas bubbles on the skin. Your companion is becoming confused, sweats heavily and develops a rapid heartbeat.
- After some frantic repairs, the car becomes more or less roadworthy. You drive frantically, rightly suspecting that your companion's life is at risk.
- Finally, you arrive at a medical centre. After some quick tests, the medical staff identify your companion as suffering from gas gangrene, caused by the bacterium *clostridium perfringens* infecting the open wound. It will be fatal unless immediate remedial action is taken. Amputation of the entire leg is a serious possibility; death cannot be ruled out.

Pause to appreciate how devastated you are by the situation. You are about to lose the person who means most to you. And you will feel responsible for that death, in that you crashed the car. Now real the sense of relief and joy you would feel when, after further examination, you are told that they are confident that it can be cured by removing the infected flesh and administering large doses of penicillin.

There is no doubt that many who would have died from gas gangrene – the most vicious of the three forms of gangrene commonly encountered – have had their lives saved by penicillin. Can you appreciate the joy that this would bring you? It brings a new depth to the old song we have just noted:

> There is a balm in Gilead
> To make the wounded whole;
> There is a balm in Gilead
> To heal the sin–sick soul.

Yet we need to take this imaginary scenario still further, in order to make one point crystal clear. Think yourself back into that situation, and let the following pointers guide you to your conclusion.

1   The medical staff prescribe immediate and aggressive treatment with penicillin G, which they begin at once. They also begin removing as much dead and infected tissue as they can. While this is going on, your thoughts turn to the penicillin that they are administering to your companion.
2   Before this incident, you had heard of penicillin and knew vaguely that it was some kind of antibiotic. But it didn't seem to be relevant to you. It held no interest for you. You knew about it, but did not see it as being of any significance for you.
3   Now, your attitude is completely different. Your companion's

life depends upon this antibiotic. You have to trust it. Without it, there is no hope.

4   The drug has the potential to heal. Yet it will not heal your companion until it is administered. If it remains in its container, it will continue to have the potential to heal your companion – but it will not do so unless and until it is administered.

The benefits which Christ won for us have indeed the potential to transform us; nevertheless, if they remain external to us – as things we know *about*, rather than know in our experiences – they cannot cure us. The balm of Gilead must be applied to our sin-sick soul if we are to be healed. At the last supper, Christ gave bread to his disciples and instructed them to 'take and eat' it (Matthew 26:26). They were to do this in remembrance of him. That pattern of 'taking and eating' applies also to the entire scheme of salvation. What Christ has won, we must make our own by faith. We must take and eat of the bread of life. The healing that Christ offers is to be accepted and received; only then can it begin its great work of renewal and restoration.

20

The benefits and the person of Christ

Reflection on the benefits which Christ brings can be immensely helpful in deepening the quality of our faith. Yet it is only right to note some difficulties which may emerge. One is that we conceive the 'benefits of Christ' as an abstraction – that is, as ideas. Instead of knowing the person of Christ, we begin to think in terms of *knowing about* what he has done for us. We begin to talk of 'forgiveness', 'redemption' or 'eternal life' – all wonderful words, it is true, but potentially *abstract* words. And we forget to talk very specifically about Jesus Christ as the one who makes these gifts possible.

Yet there is a second danger, which is much more troublesome. So often, we want to have the gift without knowing the giver. We welcome the benefits that Christ brings us, but hold back from intimacy with Christ himself. We gladly receive salvation and eternal life from Christ, as we might a gift from an elderly relative. But we don't want to spend time with him. We're too busy for that.

I remember reading a story in a newspaper about an elderly gentleman who had accumulated a fortune through business deals. He had never married and had no immediate family. He decided to give a large part of his fortune to his nephews and nieces. But there was a condition attached. They would have to visit him regularly. He wanted to get to know the people he was supporting in this way.

The nephews and nieces didn't like this very much. They had no problems about receiving the cash. Yet their uncle – who they had not seen for years – had a reputation as a cantankerous old man, with hardly any friends. Those few he had not bored to death he had alienated in some other unmentionable ways. Who would want to spend time with such a tedious old bore? In the end, of course, the lure of riches helped them to overcome this reluctance.

This pattern can be seen on a larger scale throughout human culture. Many countries name cities after the heroes who achieved their liberation from colonial powers or invading forces. Yet knowing what a hero achieved does not tell us what the hero is like as a person, as an individual who we come to know. The Victorian period saw massive expansion of British influence throughout the world, often through the use of military and naval power. Polite Victorian society was prepared to honour the achievements of the senior members of its armed forces, but privately regarded them as tedious bores. They might have achieved much, but they were generally seen as unimpressive people. Much the same was true of the great Victorian entre-preneurs who pioneered Britain's rise to dominance in the global marketplace from about 1830 onwards. Many were prepared to share in the benefits which these individuals brought to them, but still despised them as people.

There is clearly a potential spiritual problem here. We may well be delighted to accept the offer of eternal life. Yet the idea of spending quality time with Christ might seem less attractive. Instead, we could be out evangelising people, attending important church meetings or running Bible studies. Spending time with Christ seems a terrible waste of precious time. And through thinking such thoughts, we realise that we have fallen into a pit we have dug for ourselves. We want to do things for Christ, but not to be with him. We are glad to receive from him, but do not want to develop an intimate relationship with him. Something is wrong here – seriously wrong.

It is important to appreciate the great benefits which Christ won for us. Yet contemplation of the 'trophies of his grace' must never be allowed to distract us from contemplating his face and cultivating acquaintance with him. It is fatally easy to force an artificial and deeply destructive divide between the person and benefits of Christ. It is essential to love both the giver and the gifts, and not make any attempt to separate them or see them in isolation from each other.

As I thought about this problem and realised how easily I fell into the trap I have just explained, I found it helpful to let my imagination build up a picture of Christ dying on the cross. Sometimes I would just read the passion narratives and allow this picture to build up naturally; at others, I would use some of the great works of art which depict the crucifixion as windows of contemplation, allowing me to focus my thoughts upon the suffering Saviour. Then I would allow the following five words to become a framework for my thoughts:

He did this for me.

I would repeat this, pausing after each word and allowing that word to crystallise my thoughts.

1   **HE** – that is, Christ. At the heart of all my reflections, prayers and meditations must be the person of Jesus Christ. My faith focuses on him, and my spiritual growth depends upon nourishing and fostering my personal relationship with him. 'Christ' cannot be left out of 'Christianity'. I must therefore work to ensure that my life and thought centre upon him.

2   **DID** – that is, went to the cross. Christ's love for me is shown in action, in something that he actively did. The use of this verb reminds me that I am dealing with a Saviour

who actively chose to enter into this world, taking upon himself its sorrows, sin and pain.

3   **THIS** – that is, suffer and die upon the cross. This allows me to focus upon his death upon the cross, trying to take in every aspect of its significance. I would let my mind wander over Christ's betrayal, arrest, trial, humiliation and scourging. I would picture him trudging to the place of execution, so weakened that he was unable to carry his own cross. Then I would take in the way in which he was reviled, mocked and scorned as he suffered. Finally, he died. This process of reflection is a deeply moving thing to do, and it needs to be done. It prevents us from ever losing sight of the critical place of Christ in our faith and devotion.

4   **FOR** – that is, what happened was purposeful. It was no accident. This was something that had been planned and took place with Christ's knowledge and consent. The cross was part of the means by which God chose to redeem his people. Even this scene of apparent despair and hopelessness was used by God for a greater good.

5   **ME** – that is, this frail and rather unimportant person I know so well. All that I had surveyed in my mind was for me. It is a troubling yet immensely reassuring thought. Why should he want to do this for someone like me? I cannot tell. I just know that he did, and that I cannot thank him enough for doing so.

The link between those words 'he' and 'me' is thus the cross.

In this section, we have been considering some of the great benefits that Christ won for us through his life, death and resurrection. Those benefits were gained for us, and we must ensure that we drink deeply at the well opened up for us by the Lord. To know Christ is indeed to know his benefits, just as it is also to know the tranquillity of his living presence in our souls.

PART 6

Barriers to knowing Christ

Knowing Christ is not something that happens naturally. It is a gift, which needs to be received. It is a seed, which needs to be planted in order that it may grow to its full stature and achieve its potential. It is a privileged relationship, which must never be taken for granted but must be cherished and nurtured.

Up to this point, we have been considering ways of making the best use of our God-given resources to deepen our knowledge of Christ. One of the great insights of the gospel is that our longing for Christ is something that is inspired by God, and can only be fulfilled through God's grace. This point is made in a famous 'Prayer to Christ' by Anselm of Canterbury (c. 1033–1109):

> Give me what you have made me want;
> Grant that I may attain to love you as much as you command.
> I praise and thank you for the desire that you have inspired . . .
> Perfect what you have begun,
> and grant me what you have made me long for.[20]

These words express the fundamental point that our longing to know Christ is a divine gift, as is the means by which we can come to know Christ. As Anselm points out, prayer is an essential aspect of our quest for a deeper knowledge of Christ. We must ask God to perfect what he has begun, and to grant us more fully what he has caused us to desire.

So what can we do to know Christ better? One of the classic answers given by Christian writers runs like this: *we must remove barriers to knowing Christ*. Alan of Lille (died 1202) offered a visual aid which I first came across in 1979, and have since found very helpful in appreciating this point. Imagine, Alan suggests, a darkened room within a house. The room is dark because a shutter has been placed across the room's only window. Outside, the sun is blazing, yet the room remains dark because the illumination of the sun is prevented from entering the room.

If I were to remove the shutter, the brilliant sunlight would stream into the room and illuminate it. My role in this would simply have been that of removing an obstacle to sunlight. The light of the sun was already there; all that I would have done would be to allow it access to the room.

In the same way, the radiance of the risen and ascended Christ constantly illuminates us. He is the 'sun of righteousness' who will 'rise with healing in its wings' (Malachi 4:2). Yet if Christ is to illuminate the interior of our souls, we must remove the barriers which prevent it from gaining access. This image of the soul as a castle with many rooms was popularised by Teresa of Ávila (1515–82), who encouraged her readers to think of themselves as mansions with many rooms, each of which needed remodelling and redecoration. Shutters must be removed if the dark rooms of our soul are to be illuminated by Christ's healing and renewing presence. Or, to change analogies: we must open the door to allow Christ into our lives (Revelation 3:20). By doing so, we remove the barrier which prevents him gaining access to our lives.

So what barriers are we talking about? Some of these are easy to identify, if less easy to deal with – such things as pride, arrogance and downright rebelliousness. Yet other obstacles are more subtle, and pose just as great a threat to knowing Christ. I have found it useful to list things which seemed to get in the way of a closer walk with Christ, and the strategies I developed to cope with them. This section aims to identify some barriers to knowing Christ and offer some approaches which others might find helpful in wrestling with these same issues.

21

Valuing lesser things
above Christ

For Paul, nothing could be compared to knowing Christ. Everything else was shown up to be inadequate in the light of that incomparable privilege (Philippians 3:7–9). Whatever he had counted precious now seemed to him to be worthless rubbish. It was not that what he previously valued was worthless – far from it. It was simply that he now knew something better.

In 1975, I travelled to Iran with a colleague. We spent several weeks touring the country. The heat of the sun was such that it was impossible to travel between major cities by coach during daylight hours. The Iranian coach companies arranged their schedules so that long-distance travel took place in the cool of the night. Coaches would leave cities such as Isfahan or Shiraz at about ten at night, and would arrive at their destinations around dawn.

We set out from Shiraz one night for the eastern city of Kerman, close to the border with Pakistan. The skies were totally cloudless, and as the night progressed the stars seemed to shine with an almost supernatural brilliance. As the coach neared a deserted caravanserai, it became clear that there was a problem. The ancient diesel engine began to make ominous coughing noises. Finally, the coach ground to a halt while the driver tried to work out what was the matter.

The forty or so passengers got off and wandered around the ruins of the caravanserai. Apparently it had been an important staging post for traders in the previous century, and some were curious to explore its many rooms. I was fascinated by something else, however. Having lived for many years in English cities, I had rarely witnessed the spectacular glory of the night sky. The lights of English cities prevent the sky from ever becoming really dark at night, and the high level of atmospheric pollution prevented the stars from being seen in their full glory. Yet in the stillness of a remote and silent desert, the stars seemed astonishingly brilliant. I was overwhelmed with a sense of wonder.

I knew that the brilliance of the stars would vanish with the dawn as a greater light overwhelmed them. The stars would remain in the heavens, but would be transcended in brilliance by the orb of the sun. I imagine that Paul's sense of the unsurpassable richness of Christ was to the sun what his worldly achievements were to the stars.

But what if I failed to appreciate the full value of knowing Christ? What if I were to prefer the stars to the sun? Christian spiritual writers often commented on the serious threat to spiritual growth posed by preferring the lesser rather than the greater. As I immersed myself in the spiritual literature of the Middle Ages, I found this topic being discussed at great length. What, I found myself asking, could I do to avoid allowing anything to compete with Christ? How could I continue to value knowing Christ above all things and avoid prizing lesser things?

As I explored this issue, I came across a landmark treatise: *On Loving God*, written by Bernard of Clairvaux (1090–1153). This offered advice on sustaining the supremacy of the divine. Bernard writes movingly of the sense of longing of God that we ought to experience:

The believing soul longs and faints for God; she rests sweetly in the contemplation of him. She glories in the reproach of the cross, until the glory of his face shall be revealed. Like the Bride, the dove of Christ, that is covered with silver wings (Psalm 68:13), white with innocence and purity, she takes her rest in the thought of your abundant kindness, Lord Jesus. Above all, she longs for that day when in the joyful splendour of your saints, gleaming with the radiance of the Beatific Vision, her feathers shall be like gold, resplendent with the joy of your face.[21]

Immediately, I found myself sustained by these words. Bernard was encouraging his readers to anticipate the permanency and the supremacy of knowing God. All else would fade and pass away. All else would become old and stale, losing its ability to enthral and excite. Knowing God was different.

Without doubt, the temptation to place other things or people above Christ was a serious barrier to knowing him fully. Yet Bernard's words seemed to offer me a way of dealing with this difficulty. I read more of Bernard's reflections on the privilege of knowing God, especially his musings on who could be said to love God truly:

It is those who can say with truth, 'My soul refuses comfort' (Psalm 77:2). For it is appropriate that those who are not satisfied by the present should be sustained by the thought of the future; and that the contemplation of eternal happiness should console those who refuse to drink from the river of transitory joys. This is the generation of those who seek the Lord – those who seek the face of the God of Jacob, not their own. To those that long for the presence of the living God, the thought of Him is the sweetest of all things. Yet it does not satisfy; it merely increases our appetite for more, as the Scripture declares: 'they that eat me shall still be hungry' (Ecclesiasticus 24:21); as one who was hungry put it:

'When I awake up after your likeness, I shall be satisfied with it.'

Challenged by these words, I began to devise strategies for dealing with this barrier. The one that seemed to work best for me was to focus on the theme of *erosion*. What distracted me from Christ was something transient and passing, which could never satisfy me for the rest of my life. In some ways, this approach is a Christian variant on 'the grass is always greener on the other side of the fence'. It stresses the known and permanent joy of knowing Christ against the transience of all other joys that the world can offer.

I would use the following biblical verse as the basis of my reflections: 'The grass withers, the flower fades; but the word of our God will stand for ever' (Isaiah 40:8). The historical context is the coming deliverance of the people of Jerusalem from their exile in Babylon in the sixth century before Christ. The point being made is that the Babylonian empire, seemingly eternal and all-powerful, was about to crumble. The people of Jerusalem would be liberated. What seemed permanent would fade and pass away. The imagery of grass withering and flowers fading spoke powerfully of the transience of the attraction of the world. The lure of the lesser good could not be sustained. It might attract for a time; yet, like the beauty of a rare flower, it would fade. What I had to do was to realise how the lure of Christ was far greater. Not only was it intrinsically superior to anything that the world could offer, it would endure for ever.

I therefore began to argue with myself, trying to make the following points to the lower side of my nature, which seemed determined to drag me down into the world:

1   Something worldly may seem very attractive in the short term. But will it last? Won't you get bored with it? Won't it fade or rust (Matthew 6:19–21)? Isn't it part of the pattern of the experience of life that things which seemed attractive

from a distance prove considerably less so when we finally possess them? God transcends these. He will endure where all else will fade.

2   As God made the world, everything in it is a reflection of him as its creator. Sometimes that reflection is distant, sometimes it is distorted. Why settle for the reflection, when the reality is available? Every longing we possess is a secret longing for God. We may accidentally attach this longing to something or someone else – but only God, whose reflections and shadows these are, can really satisfy us.

I was able to achieve some insight into my own weaknesses in this way. Yet Christianity affirms the importance of the body of Christ as a means of spiritual growth. Others can help us grow, not least by identifying the barriers to growth which they can perceive within us and to which we may be blind. A willingness to listen to others is essential to spiritual growth – so much so that a refusal to take criticism must be regarded as a serious barrier to knowing Christ more fully. We shall explore this further in what follows.

22

An inability to take criticism

Few of us have the remarkable gift of being able to see ourselves as we really are. As many psychologists have pointed out, we have a tendency, through defence mechanisms, to think that we are perfect, popular and appreciated. This can blind us to the fact that we are actually not like that at all, preventing us from discovering ways of becoming better people and knowing Christ more fully. Criticism can be a helpful way of discovering how things really are in order that we can begin to do something about it. We prefer to see ourselves as we imagine we are, or as we would like to be – failing to realise that we often fall short of these ideals. Arrogance, all would agree, is a barrier to knowing Christ. But how do I know whether I am arrogant or not? Do I have the discernment necessary to realise that this is a problem for me?

One of the means by which we can gain a better and more realistic understanding of ourselves is by listening to the perspectives of others. Sometimes this takes the form of affirmation. It helps to know when we get things right, or when we behave in ways that others believe to be appropriate to our Christian calling.

Yet sometimes we may have to hear harsh words about

ourselves. And because these are difficult opinions to hear, we sometimes try to deny their validity. 'He never liked me, and this is just his way of trying to humiliate me.' 'She knows nothing. I don't have to listen to her.' Yet the criticisms that are being made might well be both valid and important, holding the key to our spiritual development. An inability to receive criticism is a significant barrier to knowing Christ.

It is important to acknowledge that criticism is easy to give and hard to take. There are times when personal criticism seems to be a way in which other people try to destroy our sense of self-worth. Granted, criticism can easily become a means of scoring points off people, making those who give it feel good about themselves and those who unwillingly receive it feel utterly worthless and demoralised. But this is not how it should be.

Criticism can be a vital stimulus to self-examination and personal growth. It is an essential element of Christian pastoral ministry, in which those who minister are able to help those for whom they care to discover their strengths and weaknesses and do something about them. We all need an outside perspective if we are to discover how people really feel about us, instead of relying upon our own biased and distorted perceptions of what we are like.

Criticism, then, is potentially a means of spiritual growth. But it can easily be abused. The harsh, uncaring and insensitive critic can destroy the person they are meant to be helping to grow.

Criticism implies commitment to the other person. Criticism is a privilege, which demands that the one who judges is deeply committed to the well-being and spiritual growth of the one who is being judged. Criticism must be seen as a sign and consequence of mutual care and commitment within the Christian body, and must be undertaken responsibly.

Do not judge, so that you may be not judged. For with the judgment you make you will be judged, and the measure you give will be the measure you get. Why do you see the speck in your neighbour's eye, but do not notice the log in your own eye? Or how can you say to your neighbour, 'Let me take the speck out of your eye,' when the log is in your own eye? You hypocrite, first take the log out of your own eye, and then you will see clearly to take the speck out of your neighbour's eye.

(Matthew 7:1–5)

With these words, Christ reminds us that the way we treat others will be reflected in the manner in which God treats us.

Criticism is easily understood as something that is negative. In everyday use, the word has a generally hostile tone, implying that something is being said which implies disapproval. *Criticism must be set within the context of affirmation.* I first realised this when reflecting on the crucifixion, noticing that Christ both affirms us and criticises us from the cross.

On the one hand, the cross discloses to us the full extent of God's love for us. 'God so loved the world that he gave his only Son' (John 3:16). The cross is thus the supreme demonstration of the love of God for us, demonstrating that we are dealing with a God who demonstrates his love in actions, rather than merely in words. On the other hand, Christ criticises us from the cross. We learn that we are sinners, who have chosen to go our own ways and set our own agendas. Although God loves us as we are, we are not what he would like us to be. We are thus challenged to become more like Christ. The cross brings home to us the fact that we are all under the power of sin and are unrighteous in the sight of God (Romans 3:9–10). None of us measures up to what God wants us to be. In the cross of Christ, we see judgement being passed upon us.

Christ thus directs a loving criticism towards us from his cross. It is a criticism tinged with sorrow and grounded in his over-whelming compassion for us. Christ affirms us by showing us how much we matter to him, even as he tells us that we are at best pale shadows of what he would like us to be. Yet it is easier to take this powerful criticism, knowing that Christ loves and cares for us. He criticises us because he cares for us, and passionately yearns for us to be restored and redeemed. He breaks us down, in order to build us up and lead us onwards.

This helps us understand how we should give and receive criticism. Criticism should spring out of love for those who are dear to us. We should not criticise anyone because we hope to humiliate or score cheap points against them. Criticism is to be seen as an expression of love and commitment, and a willingness to uphold and sustain the other person as they try to change and grow. Even if offered with the best of intentions, criticism can easily destroy someone's frail sense of worth and dignity, often maintained with the greatest of difficulty under adverse circumstances. Thoughtless criticism can, quite simply, be destructive and negative. And just as Christ affirms us as he judges us, so we must take care to encourage, affirm and value those to whom we minister and those for whom we care.

The final point which I found helpful was the realisation that *criticism is not an end in itself.* It is the means to the end of growth and development. Christ does not judge us in order to humiliate us and leave us battered and demoralised. The proper function of wise and caring criticism is to help people to grow and mature, discovering the gifts that God has given them, and enabling them to make the most of them in his service. The Parable of the Talents (Matthew 25:14–30) points to the fact that every believer has been gifted by God. It is vitally important that those gifts be identified and used to the full. Yet it is often difficult for individuals to identify their own gifts. An outside perspective is often essential. And it is here that a critic – in the best sense of the word – can be of real value. The outsider can help that person discover what his or her gifts are, as well as what they are *not.*

As I have grown older, I have become increasingly willing to receive criticism and less ready to give it. Why? I am more willing to receive criticism because I have become aware that my colleagues and friends have my own good in mind when they point out my weaknesses. Their intention is to help me deal with my frailties, not score points off me. I have found it easier to recognise the love and concern which lies behind their comments. And I am less ready to criticise anyone because I believe that criticism implies a willingness to support someone as they try to change. As a result, I only criticise when I feel it is absolutely necessary. I hope that this means that I am a nicer person than I used to be!

More importantly, a willingness to listen to others defeats the grand strategy of sin – that we deceive ourselves, believing we are something we are not. Being open to the judgements of others prevents us from being deceived by our natural sinful tendency to believe that we are perfect, and need not trouble ourselves over such potentially difficult matters as personal holiness and spiritual growth. Through God's grace, others can help us identify our weaknesses, and support and encourage us as we try to deal with them. The journey of faith is not, and was never meant to be, a solitary walk into the future. We travel in the company of the saints, and have the privilege of mutual support and care throughout the long journey to the New Jerusalem.

23

Not being willing to grow

Faith is like a seed, planted in the earth, which grows into a plant. This familiar image, found in many of the parables of the kingdom, points to the dynamic nature of the Christian life. Like a mustard seed (Mark 4:31–2), faith grows from small beginnings. It is something which is in a process of transition. Paul develops this analogy a little further, pointing out that God is deeply involved in this process of development. One person may plant the seed, another may water it – but God is the one who makes it grow (1 Corinthians 3:6–7).

For our purposes, what really matters is that *seeds grow*. If a seed is not growing, it is probably sterile or dead. *Growth is about change*. It involves letting go in order to grow. Yet some Christians feel profoundly uneasy with the idea of change. They prefer the safety and security of the past. Sometimes a theological justification for a refusal to develop is offered. 'I first heard the gospel from Pastor Smith. If I depart from anything he told me, I'm not really a Christian.' Others are aware that a certain person played a hugely important role in their growth as Christians – perhaps a pastor, friend or relative. As they were so helpful and supportive, we feel the need to replicate their vision of Christianity. The prime goal of Christian discipleship becomes to imitate someone else's personal faith, in terms of both its content and its commitment.

It is easy to understand the concerns expressed in this way. The issue of personal loyalty is immensely important here. Some Christians believe that to move beyond what they were told of the gospel at the time of their conversion is to invalidate their coming to faith. To develop deeper ways of knowing Christ than that offered by Pastor Smith is about believing in a different gospel. Pastor Smith may well have warned you about this: 'Don't deviate from anything I told you!'

One person may evangelise us; another may help us to get going properly on the journey of faith. The evangelist and spiritual mentor both have their place in God's good purposes. But it is essential not to confuse the person who introduced us to Christ, or helped us deepen our walk with him, with Christ himself. Without realising what is happening, we can allow Christianity to be *defined* by a person – whereas in fact all that they did was to *introduce* Christ to us. It is fatally easy to equate spiritual growth with mimicking the ideas of someone who was very helpful to us. Yet this can easily degenerate into knowing Christ indirectly – that is, by trying to enter into a personal experience and understanding of Christ which reflects the God-given identity of someone else. Christ longs to deal with us as individuals. He does not want to relate to us through surrogates, but wants to establish his transforming presence within each of us.

Think of a person who has become very important to you. Now imagine that the two of you were introduced by a mutual friend. That friend clearly played an important role. He made the connection between the two of you. But once you have encountered the other person, that relationship begins to develop its own momentum and distinctive character. You begin to know this special person more deeply – perhaps even more deeply than the friend who originally brought you together. Your relationship grows. And precisely because it grows, it changes.

Is that really such a frightening thought? The person who introduced you played a critically important and even indispensable role. But in the end, what sustains and stimulates the relationship is not the person who introduced you but the person to whom you were introduced. As you come to know and love them more deeply, the relationship grows and deepens. *A static relationship is a dead relationship.* Growth in a relationship is a sign of life.

Evangelism can be thought of as planting the seed of faith in someone's life (1 Corinthians 3:6–7). The person who planted it has played their role, and must be honoured for it. Likewise, there are others who will water that seed and help it to grow. But the gospel seed has a God-given life of its own, and it is critically important to allow that seed to grow in our lives as it pleases, rather than stunt its growth by demanding that it mimics precisely what we find in other Christians we admire. This kind of undue reliance on others is a serious barrier to knowing Christ fully, and it must be identified and confronted. We cannot allow the quality of our relationship with Christ to be constricted in this way. Christ demands to be known as he is and as he wishes, not as one of his well-meaning servants dictates.

This is a difficult and painful issue which will not go away and cannot be ignored. The person who brought us to faith, or mentored us at a crucially important juncture in our spiritual journey, may have played their role well, and to the full. Yet that may be where their influence should end. I have seen too many lives of faith stunted by the inappropriate continuing influence of voices from the past, as those who were faithful servants to young Christians demanded to be their masters, seeming to place personal loyalty to them and their beliefs above allowing a full and living relationship with Christ to flourish. 'This is how *I* know Christ; therefore this is how *you* should know Christ.' The New Testament asks that we conform to Christ; some Christian leaders ask that we conform to them instead. This is not acceptable, and must be resisted.

In thinking about this difficult and occasionally painful question, I have found it genuinely helpful to identify all those who have helped me in some way along the Christian way. There are many such people, and some of them will probably never know how much I owe them. The book I read; the sermon I heard; the casual conversation over lunch – all have proved important in helping me along the road of faith. I then try to identify three things about each of them:

- the ways in which they have helped me;
- their strengths;
- their weaknesses.

Let me stress that it is *not* dishonouring to any of those who have helped us to suggest that they have weaknesses. Precisely because we are fallen and frail creatures, we are all prone to these. The real problems arise when people refuse to acknowledge that they have any weaknesses!

I then thank God for these people, holding them up before him and praying for any special needs which they may have. In particular, I give thanks for the help they have been to me, and for the many gifts which he has given them. I would then ask that I might have the humility to learn from their weaknesses, as well as their strengths.

I found that this approach allowed me to honour and respect those who have helped me in such important ways, without setting them on pedestals or making them into plaster saints. I could identify which aspects of their thinking and lives I should appropriate, and which I should overlook.

As we have seen, the guidance and support of others is critical for the journey of faith. The two key errors that we can make are to ignore others (by refusing to be open to their insights and criticisms) or to venerate them (and thus placing them between ourselves and Christ, so that they obscure him and cause us to over-esteem their judgements). There is a middle way here, which is open to the judgements of others, yet ultimately accountable only to Christ. Our fellow travellers serve us best when they catalyse our relationship with Christ, not when they deliberately or unintentionally usurp his place as the Lord of our lives and guardian of our souls.

24

Falling in love with the world

Christ came into this world to bring us out of it. That, in a nutshell, is the essence of the Christian hope. Like the great saints of old, we know that we have no abiding city on earth but are bound for the New Jerusalem. On account of Christ we are citizens of heaven and await our entry into the heavenly realms with eager anticipation. However, we must live out the remainder of our lives in this world, in which we are called to serve Christ and to witness to him. We are citizens of heaven, and sojourners on earth.

It is at this point that a serious barrier to knowing Christ may develop. We can see ourselves as citizens of this world, with little more than a passing interest in heaven. We become like travellers who, passing through a strange land on our way to our final destination, fall in love with the land through which we pass. The destination becomes forgotten as the traveller becomes a settler. This world is our place of exile, from which we shall return to the New Jerusalem. Yet it is important to recall that some of the inhabitants of Jerusalem who were deported to Babylon in Old Testament times came to prefer their place of exile to their native land, and chose not to return home when Babylon fell to the conquering Persians.

Falling in love with the world can seriously prejudice our relationship with Christ. Before exploring this further, let us be clear that knowing Christ does not in any way conflict with longing to serve God in the world, take its pain and sorrows seriously and make it a better place. The doctrine of the incarnation reminds us that God chose to lodge himself within the realities and structures of this world in order to redeem it, and we must try to mirror this divine compassion for and commitment to the world. When I was a student, I remember a slogan that was widely cited in Christian circles: 'Don't be so heavenly minded that you are no earthly use!' Like most memorable slogans, this mingled a little bit of truth with a lot of nonsense. To love Christ *is* to love the world, precisely because Christ loves that world, and we who love him must love what he loves. Yet loving Christ takes absolute priority here, and provides the ultimate motivation for our concern for this tired and weary world in which we live. We love the world because Christ loved it first (John 3:16), and longs to redeem it. Believing that we may have a role in that process, we love what our Saviour loves, in order that all may know him and be reconciled to him.

I spent a lot of my time as a young Christian wrestling with the question of how best to understand the relationship between Christ and the world. Could I love one without loving the other? How could I make sure that I did not fall in love with my place of exile, rather than eagerly anticipate what the future held for me and the whole pilgrim people of God? Three main patterns of relating to the world can be discerned within the long Christian tradition of spiritual reflection. Reflecting on their strengths and weaknesses was an important part of my personal growth in faith.

The rejection of the world

This approach holds that the world is a place of contamination and fallenness. Christian believers should avoid any such defilement or pollution by ensuring that they avoid contact with the world. Two strategies are usually advocated. First, believers are encouraged to withdraw physically from the everyday world. The 'Desert Fathers', such as Alexander of Egypt, left the cities behind and established communities in the desert, free from the moral and spiritual pollution which they feared would compromise their spiritual integrity. The monastic movement, which reached its zenith in the Middle Ages, generally held that the integrity of faith was best pre-served by surrounding the Christian community with stone walls and enclosing each believer within a cell. In this way, the purity of faith could be maintained.

Second, an attitude of contempt for the world was encouraged. This can be seen clearly in the title of one of the best-loved works of medieval spirituality – Thomas à Kempis's *The Imitation of Christ and Contempt for the World*, written in the fifteenth century. It was argued that it was impossible to be a first-class Christian and remain in the world. That option was only available for the lowest class of believer. The spiritual élite would have nothing to do with the world, and took pride (in the best possible sense of the word, of course) in disdaining it.

I could see that this attitude had something to commend it. Many Christians do find it difficult to cope with the world, and this solution to that problem certainly offered some interesting possibilities. Yet I also found myself deeply concerned over its attitude to the world. To know Christ is to long to proclaim Christ. And how can the wonders of Christ be proclaimed to the world if you have rejected any contact with that world? The biblical images of believers as 'salt of the earth' and 'light of the world' (Matthew 5:13–14) both pointed to the need for believers to be *noticed* within the world, in order to be able to convey the good news of the kingdom.

I also found myself worried by this stridently negative attitude towards the world. Yes, the world is fallen. But it remains God's creation. How can I hate something that God has created and longs to restore to himself? After all, God loved that world so much that he gave his only Son for it (John 3:16). For these reasons, therefore, I began to explore taking a more positive attitude towards the world.

Embracing the world

One of my keenest interests is the history and thought of the European Reformation. This great period in European cultural history is of no small importance to Christian spirituality. Writers such as Martin Luther (1483–1546) and John Calvin (1509–64) encouraged Christians to live out their lives in the world. The idea of a spiritual élite, confined within monastery walls, was vigorously rejected. Christianity was a faith of the marketplace, in which believers were called to lead their lives. Later interpreters of the Reformation argued that Christians should embrace the world and immerse themselves in its affairs.

Initially, I found myself persuaded by this wholesale affirmation of the world. It offered the possibility of making Christ known to the world through being present as an active participant in that world. Yet my initial enthusiasm for the approach soon cooled. Those who speak enthusiastically of 'embracing the world' generally end up being embraced by the world and losing their Christian distinctiveness. To live as an active participant in the world can easily slide into accepting a secular ethos, which has no genuine place for Christ. This approach seemed to ignore the fact that the world can be a hostile place for faith. Many of the nineteenth-century writers who commended this approach lived and worked within an explicitly Christian culture, whether in Europe or North America. Things have changed, with western culture becoming markedly more hostile to the public profession of Christian faith in the workplace.

I therefore began to wonder if there was a more realistic

approach to knowing Christ which would foster engagement with the world, allowing Christ to be proclaimed, while sustaining a personal relationship with Christ and avoiding erosion of Christian distinctiveness. A closer reading of Luther and Calvin helped me to realise that they had been misrepresented by some of their later interpreters. Both writers were indeed concerned to ensure that the Christian faith was a living and dynamic presence in the marketplace. Yet they were also aware of the threat that sustained exposure to the world could cause to faith, and sought to develop ways of sustaining faith within the world. I later found similar ideas in the writings of Augustine. In what follows, I shall outline this approach, which I believe to be a viable and helpful framework for knowing Christ while serving him in this world.

A critical engagement with the world

The basic principle I found through my close and attentive reading of Augustine, Luther and Calvin is that of a critical engagement with the world – that is, of being present and active in the world, while realising that the world is not 'neutral' in matters of faith. It can easily drag us down and come between Christ and the believer. I began to realise that the world can exist in a double configuration for Christians. On the one hand, it is the creation of God, which he loves. On the other, it is a fallen realm, which poses a threat to faith. This tension can be clearly seen in John's Gospel, which uses the same term, 'world', to refer both to the creation which God loves (e.g., John 3:16) and to the rebellious and sinful domain with the potential to engulf and overwhelm us (John 17:13–15).

Don't conform – transform! Christians are called to be in the world but not of the world; to be a transforming presence within the world – like yeast in dough – without conforming to its ways of thinking and doing. 'Do not be conformed to this world but be transformed by the renewing of your minds'

(Romans 12:2). Knowing Christ offers us a framework for a constructive yet critical engagement with the world, allowing us to journey usefully in hope, looking forward to finally being with Christ for ever.

PART 7

How Christ is to be known

As I am Irish, I suppose that it is only natural that I should have a special interest in St Patrick, the patron saint of Ireland. Indeed, one of my few claims to fame is that I was baptised in the cathedral built on the site of Saint Patrick's grave. Patrick is traditionally regarded as the author of the hymn known as either 'St Patrick's breastplate' or 'The deer's cry'. This hymn stresses the importance of personally binding the power of God and the great truths of the gospel to oneself. One of its verses focuses on the importance of grasping and personally apprehending every aspect of Christ's life, death and resurrection. The words of one of its early verses read as follows:

> I bind this day to me for ever,
> By power of faith, Christ's incarnation;
> His baptism in Jordan river;
> His death on Cross for my salvation;
> His bursting from the spicèd tomb;
> His riding up the heavenly way;
> His coming at the day of doom;
> I bind unto myself today.[22]

Everything that Christ did and everything that was done to Christ *was for our benefit*. Christ did not simply die; he died for us, and for our salvation. To know Christ is to become aware of the critical importance of every aspect of his identity ministry for our journey of faith. We must savour everything he said and did, knowing that it is packed with spiritual significance.

There are times when it is important to stand back from the life and ministry of Christ and appreciate him as a totality – the big picture, as opposed to its individual brush strokes. Yet there are other times when we need to focus on its individual aspects, making sure that we have feasted on what they have to offer and to say to us. In this section, we shall pick up some of the individual themes which focus on Christ, and ask how they help us to know him better.

So in what ways can the great events and themes of Christ's ministry impact upon our hearts and minds and imaginations? In what ways can they challenge us to go further and go deeper? In what follows, we shall reflect on some of the great themes which focus on Jesus Christ, and allow them to confront the superficiality which passes for Christian faith for so many of us.

25

Knowing Christ as the fulfilment of prophecy

To know Christ is to be caught up in a heady mixture of memories and anticipations, in which both the past and the future shape and nurture our present. We remember all that God has done in the past, and look forward confidently with a sense of expectation to the future. The present often seems insecure in comparison with both past and future. Many Christians feel that it is relatively easy to be sure that God acted in the past – as in the exodus from Egypt, the birth of Christ and the resurrection. Equally, they trust that God will act in power at some time in the future, when the great scroll of history is closed and the kingdom of God finally ushered in. But what about the present?

The image of the trapeze artist has helped me make some sense of this situation. The journey of faith is like the trapeze artist in mid-air, halfway between the security of the bar she has just left and the one which she will catch hold of in a few instants. Yet for those few seconds of suspense, she is poised without support between past and future. To know Christ in the present is to look back at past securities and anticipate those which lie in the future. Faith is about journeying in hope, trusting in the God whose great acts always seem to have been experienced by other people. I sometimes feel that the best we can hope for is to know memories, shadows and reflections of past acts of greatness. Maybe it would have been easier to sustain my faith if I had been there at the parting of the Red Sea, or at the appearance of Christ to his disciples on the road to Emmaus. But that was then; this is now.

In this situation, I have found it immensely helpful to focus on knowing Christ as the fulfilment of prophecy. This way of focusing on Christ brings together past, present and future, forming a matrix which injects both promise and stability into the uncertainties and hesitations of the present. What Israel longed for, but perhaps feared would never come, was faithfully fulfilled in Christ. The encounter between the infant Christ and Simeon brings this out poignantly. It is difficult to read this narrative without being moved by the joy of an old man who found that what he and his people had longed for – and perhaps secretly feared would never happen – had been fulfilled in his lifetime and in his presence.

> Now there was a man in Jerusalem whose name was Simeon; this man was righteous and devout, looking forward to the consolation of Israel, and the Holy Spirit rested upon him. It had been revealed to him by the Holy Spirit that he would not see death before he had seen the Lord's Messiah. Guided by the Spirit, Simeon came into the temple; and when the parents brought in the child Jesus, to do for him what was customary under the law, Simeon took him in his arms and praised God, saying, 'Master, now you are dismissing your servant in peace, according to your word; for my eyes have seen your salvation, which you have prepared in the presence of all peoples, a light for revelation to the Gentiles, and for glory to your people Israel.' And the child's father and mother were amazed at what was being said about him.
>
> (Luke 2:25–33)

How do we know that we can trust God? There are many answers, some dangerously simplistic, to this pressing and often troublesome question. Yet the best answers are sometimes the simplest, as in this case. We must never lose sight of the fact that the final and supreme ground for trusting God is Christ himself. To contemplate Christ is to see the image of a faithful, compassionate and trustworthy God, totally committed to the welfare and redemption of his people. When Christ declares and promises, he speaks as one who may be trusted. Remembering all that Christ has done for us in the past and anticipating what he will do for us in the future brings a sense of tranquillity and expectation to the present, enabling us to continue the journey of faith. At times, we may be uncertain about many things. Yet we may trust the Christ who accompanies us and longs to lead us to journey's end.

These insights need to be brought home to us at the corporate, not just the individual, level. I certainly believe that Christ is the fulfilment of Old Testament prophecy, and rejoice that this is so. Yet this is also the belief of the entire people of God. It is the faith of the Church, not simply a private insight which I find helpful. One of the many issues I have been forced to work through in my own walk of faith is the role of the community of faith in spiritual development. Like many Christians, I tend to be something of an individualist in my outlook. As a result, I was blinded to many of the blessings that come from taking the corporate side of faith more seriously. I found reading Dietrich Bonhoeffer's work *Life Together* (latest edition, Augsburg Fortress, 1996) enormously helpful in this way, especially his emphasis on corporate prayer and Bible study.

Yet the worship of the Church also has a major role to play in personal spiritual growth. Its patterns of public worship can offer us a framework for private thought and reflection. I found this to be the case when pondering the theme of Christ as the fulfilment of prophecy. The church service which helped me to focus my thoughts, mingling private reflection with public praise and adoration, was the famous Service of Nine Lessons and Carols, designed to enable worshippers to grasp the full significance and joy of the Christmas message.

How did this service come into being? The Victorian period witnessed Christmas becoming a major national religious festival in England. The practice of having Christmas trees was introduced by Queen Victoria's consort, Albert, from his native Germany. Christmas cards were circulated using the newly established national postal service, making extensive use of a device invented by the novelist Anthony Trollope – the post box. The Victorian period witnessed an explosion in the writing of Christmas carols; some of the best-known carols date from this hugely influential and formative period in English history, including 'In the bleak midwinter' and 'Once in royal David's city'.

As Christmas became an increasingly important festival in the later nineteenth century, it became painfully clear that no adequate provision had been made by the English national church for celebrating it publicly. The 1662 Book of Common Prayer offered no special arrangements for the Christmas season, other than specifying certain appropriate collects and readings. As the celebration of Christmas became more and more prominent in the national consciousness, the demand grew for a special church service for this time of year, incorporating both carols and biblical readings.

One such service was first held late on Christmas Eve in the year 1880. It had been devised by Edward White Benson (1829–96) while he was bishop of the diocese of Truro, in the southwestern part of England. The format was both simple and elegant. The service consisted of nine carols and nine lessons, to be read by various officials of the church in ascending order, beginning with a chorister and ending with the bishop himself. Benson went on to become Archbishop of Canterbury; the service went on to be adopted, in a new format, at King's College, Cambridge.

It would become a national, and finally global, institution within fifty years.

The origins of the distinctive Cambridge format go back to Christmas Eve 1918, the first Christmas celebration after the trauma and devastation of the First World War. Eric Milner-White had just been appointed chaplain and dean of King's College, Cambridge, having served as an army chaplain during the war. He was acutely aware of the need to make worship more relevant and attractive to a hardened and sceptical post-war generation, and realised that the Christmas story could be used as a showcase for Christian worship. Exploiting the long-established choral tradition of King's College, Milner-White set about developing the format of the Nine Lessons and Carols. While some modifications were introduced in December 1919, the format has remained more or less the same ever since.

The backbone of the service consists of nine Christmas carols and nine biblical readings, interspersed with choral items reflecting Christmas themes. The opening words of its famous Bidding Prayer put a frame around the nine readings which will follow, and allow the congregation to appreciate to its full the biblical feast which will follow.

The Bidding Prayer

Beloved in Christ, be it this Christmas Eve our care and delight to prepare ourselves to hear again the message of the angels: in heart and mind to go even unto Bethlehem and see this thing which is come to pass, and with the shepherds and the wise men adore the Child lying in his Mother's arms. Let us read and mark in Holy Scripture the tale of the loving purposes of God from the first days of our disobedience unto the glorious Redemption brought us by this Holy Child.

The Bidding Prayer sets out the purpose of the service: 'to prepare ourselves to hear again the message of the angels: in heart and mind to go even unto Bethlehem and see this thing which is come to pass, and with the shepherds and the wise men adore the Child lying in his Mother's arms'. The biblical readings are intended to set the historical, theological and spiritual scene for the coming of Christ, so that the full significance of this event may be appreciated. Martin Luther once suggested that Scripture was 'the swaddling clothes and manger in which Christ is laid': in other words, the Bible establishes a framework by which the full relevance of the birth, death and resurrection of Christ may be understood.

The Bidding Prayer develops this point by stressing the role of the reading of the Bible in calling to mind the great events of salvation history: 'Let us read and mark in Holy Scripture the tale of the loving purposes of God from the first days of our disobedience unto the glorious Redemption brought us by this Holy Child.' The nine readings from Scripture which then follow set out the great theme of promise and fulfilment, telling of how God set about redeeming fallen humanity through the coming of Christ. The readings set out the great hopes and expectations of the Old Testament, and show how these were fulfilled in Christ.

The nine lessons

Lesson 1: Genesis 3:8–15; 17–19
Lesson 2: Genesis 22:15–18
Lesson 3: Isaiah 9:2, 6–7
Lesson 4: Isaiah 11:1–3a; 4a; 6–9
Lesson 5: Luke 1:26–35; 38
Lesson 6: Luke 2: 1, 3–7
Lesson 7: Luke 2:8–16
Lesson 8: Matthew 2:1–12
Lesson 9: John 1:1–14

I have no doubt that there are other ways in which we can grasp how the great biblical theme of prophecy, promise and fulfilment can be understood to converge on Christ. We are all individual and find different things helpful as devotional aids. Yet this service stimulates both mind and imagination. In addition to affirming the importance of reflecting on the identity of Christ, the service itself encourages imaginative reflection. It is held late in the day at a time when the northern hemisphere is wrapped in the darkness and cold of winter, helping us to imagine the state of a lost world without Christ. It is indeed a land cloaked in darkness, which longed to see a great light. And as the church is lit up, we begin to gain an understanding of the coming of Christ as the light of the world. Images and texts thus mingle together, unleashing a cascade of thoughts and reflections on the identity of Christ and his significance for our world.

One such thought, strongly affirmed by both lessons and carols in this service, is that Christ is none other than God incarnate. As the famous carol 'Hark, the herald angels sing!' – traditionally one of the core elements of this service – sets out this idea:

> Veiled in flesh the Godhead see,
> Hail the incarnate Deity!
> Pleased as man with man to dwell,
> Jesus our Emmanuel!

This naturally leads us to consider the importance of knowing Christ as God incarnate for our personal spiritual development.

26

Knowing Christ as God incarnate

One of the most dramatic insights of the Christian faith is that the God who created the heavens and the earth chose to come and dwell among us humans beings, as one of us. Let us listen as Paul shares his sense of wonder at this thought with the Christian community at Philippi:

> Though he was in the form of God, [Christ] did not regard equality with God as something to be exploited, but emptied himself, taking the form of a slave, being born in human likeness. And being found in human form, he humbled himself and became obedient to the point of death, even death on a cross.
>
> (Philippians 2:6–8)

For Paul, the idea that the sovereign and creator Lord should humble himself to this extent is as amazing as it is true. Not only does the creator of the world stoop down to enter into his creation, he enters the world as its servant, and is put to death by his creatures by the most inhuman form of execution that human ingenuity could devise. The creator and redeemer of humanity willingly suffered the fate that civilised humanity reserved for its worst criminals.

Christian theology has used the term 'incarnation' to express this stunning insight. The word literally means 'being in the flesh', and sums up the great Christian truth that 'in Christ God was reconciling the world to himself' (2 Corinthians 5:19). God did not send a subordinate to redeem us. He chose to do it himself. God himself enters into this world, the vale of soul-making, full of darkness and tragedy. The Father set out into the 'far country' to call his lost and wayward children home, so that they might feast with him.

For many Christians, the doctrine of the incarnation can be summarised succinctly in the biblical affirmation that the 'Word became flesh and lived among us' (John 1:14). The Greek word here translated by 'lived' is translated more accurately as 'pitched his tent'. This translation presents us with a powerful image of a wandering people who dwell in tents, as Israel did in the period looked back to by the prophets as a time when she was close to God. As they wander on the journey of faith, they find a new tent pitched in their midst. God himself has come to dwell among them, as they travel. God is with them in their journey of faith, as their constant companion and consoler. God truly cares for his people, not from a distance, but as a fellow traveller on the road of human life.

This is a theme which the Christian Church fondly recalls at Christmas, as it rejoices in the knowledge that its Saviour did not dismiss his people as insignificant or devoid of value. So much did our creator and redeemer love us that he chose to enter into his creation in the most lowly manner. Perhaps one of the finest and best-known statements of this theme of the self-humiliation of the redeemer is that of Mrs Cecil F. Alexander, in her carol 'Once in royal David's city':

> He came down to earth from heaven
> Who is God and Lord of all
> And his shelter was a stable
> And his cradle was a stall.

With the poor and mean and lowly
Lived on earth our Saviour holy.[23]

We do not have to climb a ladder into heaven in order to find God and be with him. God has come down that ladder, in order to meet us where we are and take us back with him. We don't have to become like God before we can encounter him. God became like us first. God meets us right where we are, without preconditions. The personal relationship that Christians presently enjoy with God through Christ is a foretaste of the fuller and deeper fellowship we will one day experience – yet which we may anticipate now.

Humanity had fallen into the gutter through its sin. Yet God did not abandon us. If we were in the gutter, God would join us there. He would abide with us, sharing our shame and pain, while making it possible for us to rise above this and finally join him in the halls of the New Jerusalem. Our Saviour came to our home in order to bring us to his home, where we may rest and feast with him.

Knowing Christ as God incarnate opens a series of windows of insight into the spiritual life, each of which deserves the most careful thought and reflection. We shall consider two, each of which helps us know Christ more fully and more intimately.

First, the incarnation allows us to picture God. To know Christ is to know God. To have seen Christ is to have seen God: 'Whoever has seen me has seen the Father' (John 14:9). Christ discloses the face of God. 'When I look into the face of Jesus, and see there the very face of God, I know that I have not seen that face elsewhere and cannot see that face elsehow' (Hugh Ross Mackintosh). Islam has much to say about doing the will of God. Yet in Christ we see and know the *face* of that God.

To appreciate the importance of this, we may reflect on the love of God. What can we say about God's love for us? How do we know what that love is like? At a very basic level, we might say that this love is infinite, boundless, beyond human telling, and so on. While this might seem promising, on closer examination it proves to be severely limited. We seem to have learned rather more about what the love of God is *not* like rather than what it *is* like. As grasping the love of God for us is such an important aspect of knowing Christ, this forces us to ask if there is a better way – a way of discerning and depicting the love of God for us which appeals to our imaginations and enables us to picture the love of God in action, not as an abstract idea.

On the basis of the doctrine of the incarnation and the many biblical insights this brings together, we may make a very positive and simple statement about the love of God for us. The love of God is like the love of someone who willingly dies for a friend (John 15:13). Here we have a moving and poignant image drawn from human experience – something concrete and tangible; something we can visualise and relate to; something that appeals to our imaginations, that generates inspirational images which can only heighten our awareness of the wonder of what God has done for us. In the picture of someone laying down his life, giving his very being for someone he loves, we have a most powerful, striking and moving statement of the full extent of the love of God for sinners. We can talk about the love of God in terms of the tender and deeply moving image of Jesus Christ trudging to Calvary, there to die for those who he loved. He did not need to do this; he *chose* to do it – and he chose to do it *for us*.

Second, the incarnation assures us that God is with us – even in the darkest moments of life. This great theme of the incarnation is summed up in the name given to Christ at his birth: 'Emmanuel' – 'God is with us' (Matthew 1:20–3). We must appreciate the importance of names for the biblical writers. Being allowed to give someone a name established your authority over them, just as the Babylonians gave new names to Daniel and his companions to indicate they were servants of the state (Daniel 1:7). In the creation accounts, it is Adam who is allowed to name the animals (Genesis 2:19–20) and thus to establish authority over them. But no human being is allowed to name God. It is God himself who reveals his name to us (Exodus 3:13–15).

The name chosen was believed to indicate the nature of the person being named. So it was with Jesus. Mary and Joseph are told what the name of their child shall be. They were not permitted to choose it themselves: 'you are to name him Jesus, for he will save his people from their sins' (Matthew 1:21). Mary and Joseph did not choose this name, as if the idea of Jesus as a potential saviour was their idea; the name was chosen for them, indicating that they were authorised to give the child this name, with all that this implied. The name 'Jesus' literally means 'God saves', just as 'Emmanuel' means 'God with us' (Matthew 1:23).

What, then, does 'God with us' mean? Two main meanings may be identified. First, *God is on our side.* 'If God is for us, who is against us?' (Romans 8:31–2). 'God is with us' means 'God is on our side'. The birth of the Son of God demonstrates and proclaims that God is on our side, that he has committed himself to the cause of the salvation of sinful humanity. In the birth of the long-promised Saviour, in his death on the cross of Calvary and in his resurrection from the dead, we have a demonstration, a proof, a guarantee, that God stands by us. Christmas tells us that the God we are dealing with, the God and Father of our Lord Jesus Christ, is not a God who is indifferent to our fate, but one who is passionately committed to our salvation, to redeeming us from sin, and to raising us to eternal life on the last day.

Second, 'God is with us' means that God *is present among us.* We are not talking of a God who stands far off from his world, aloof and distant from its problems. We are dealing with a God who has entered into our human situation, who became man and dwelt among us as one of us, someone who knows at first hand what it is like to be frail, mortal and human, to suffer and to die. We cannot explain suffering, but we can say that God took it upon himself to follow this way. He chose to suffer. At the scene of the crucifixion, the crowds standing around Jesus made fun of him. Even the soldiers sneered at him. 'If you are the King of the Jews,' they said, 'save yourself!' (Luke 23:37). But he stayed there and died, and saved us instead. One of the greatest wonders of the gospel is that God chose to save us by suffering himself.

In Christ, God came down to earth from heaven. Yet there is more to the theme of incarnation than this. In Christ, *earth is drawn up into heaven.* The light of the world shone on our earth and illuminated it, just as the darkness of our world was swallowed up and drowned in the immensity of God. Through Christ, our weariness, pain and exhaustion were brought before the throne of grace as things that God knows, not just knows about. And through that same Christ, the face of that same God is brought to us, so that we might see and know it – and long to see and know it fully at the end of this age.

So how might we apply the ideas we have considered in this section? How might we put some of these insights to use as we seek to know Christ in our personal journey of faith? At times, we feel immensely lonely. The journey of faith seems to be one of an endless and depressing solitude. We often long for companionship on that long and difficult road. The doctrine of the incarnation assures us that the God who has called us to be with him has already travelled that road. The creator has entered the creation, and knows precisely what conditions we face. God has graced the journey of life with his own personal transfiguring presence. The tears of Christ have been shed on the road of human sorrow and suffering before us. We are not alone: the creator of the world has gone ahead of us, blazing a trail for us, and waits for us to join him at journey's end.

These reflections naturally lead us on to reflect on the importance of knowing Christ as the one who was crucified for us.

27

Knowing Christ as crucified

The creator suffered at the hands of his creation. We can see here one of the greatest paradoxes of the Christian faith. So deeply was the human race enmeshed with sin that they not only failed to recognise their creator and redeemer on his entry into his world, they put him to death using one of the most sadistic and humiliating forms of execution ever devised. To understand the full significance of the crucifixion of Christ has been one of the central tasks of Christian theology and spirituality.

For Paul, the Christian faith is distinguished from both Judaism and the ideas of classical Greek culture by its proclamation of the crucifixion of Christ. Part of the task of the Christian believer is to understand the full meaning of the cross. This can be done by developing some of the great themes that the New Testament attaches to Christ's death on the cross and his resurrection in glory. The cross represents the glorious triumph of God over the forces of sin, evil and despair. It represents the breaking of the party of Satan and the bringing of new hope to the lives of believers. The cross is the foundation of authentic forgiveness – the only means by which we can be restored to fellowship with God. It represents the fullest disclosure of the overwhelming love of God for his sinful creatures, and his determination to restore us to all that he intended for us.

Yet far more is required of us than simply understanding the meaning of the cross. We have failed to appreciate the wonder of the gospel if we think of the cross of Christ as merely introducing new ideas into the world. The cross is about transformation; it is about the changing of lives. To know Christ is not simply to know that he was crucified, as a matter of history. It is to experience that crucifixion as a present reality in our own lives, in which our former ways of living are put to death and new patterns of life are made possible. The cross needs to affect our hearts as well as our minds. As many of us have found out to our cost, the mind and heart do not always connect up with each other. It is not merely important that the cross affects our hearts as well as our minds; it is *essential* that this takes place.

I personally find this thought to be very difficult and challenging. I can cope with the demand to change the way in which I think. Yet the crucified Christ beckons to me from his cross, asking me to do far more for him than simply change my ideas. He asks me to give him my life and allow him to refashion it. It may be painful, and it may take a long time – but I want him to do it. That reshaping will involve the imposing of the pattern of the cross upon my life, in that I must now expect to share in his suffering. I would find it much easier simply to accept some modest adjustment to my ideas, but what is demanded of me is much greater. Yet how can I forget that Christ did not simply bring some new ideas about God into the world? He died, slowly and painfully, to bring new possibilities into a world which had given up hope.

Ignatius Loyola (1491–1556) made a similar point powerfully in his *Spiritual Exercises*. Loyola invites me to enter into a dialogue with the dying Christ over the costliness of redemption and the love of the creator in redeeming the creation. In his *Spiritual Exercises*, Ignatius outlines an exercise in which he asks those following his directions to join him in focusing their thoughts on Christ dying on the cross. Loyola invites his readers to imagine themselves as being present at Calvary. He asks them to engage in a dialogue with the dying Christ. Initially, this involves reflection on what is happening: the creator suffering for the creation; the one who has eternal life by right choosing to suffer physical pain and death for sinners. Then this meditation is used as a means for self-examination, with a view to setting a future agenda for spiritual growth and discipline. Here are the words which I found so challenging and helpful:

> Imagine Christ our Lord before you, hanging upon the cross. Talk to him about how the creator became a human being, and how he who possesses eternal life submitted himself to physical death for our sins. Then I shall reflect on myself, and ask:

> > What I have done for Christ?
> > What I am now doing for Christ?
> > What ought I to do for Christ?

> As I see him like this, hanging upon the cross, I shall meditate on what comes to mind.[24]

The dialogue which Loyola wishes those undertaking the exercises to enter into has the effect of moving them from thought to action. I was asked to meditate on the sufferings of Christ. After I had reflected on what Christ has done for me, Loyola demanded that I ask what I was doing for Christ.

One of the reasons this was such a moving experience for me was that I was being forced to imagine discussing my understanding of Christ *in his presence*. I had always found it easy and undemanding to think about the meaning of the cross in abstract terms. I was able to adopt a detached approach, rather like talking about somebody in their absence. But this was different. The approach that Loyola asked me to take placed me uncomfortably close to the pain and suffering of my Saviour. It was as if he was looking over my shoulder, asking me what I made of his sacrifice for me and what I proposed to do for him in return. In many ways, it was a deeply shaming experience, as it brought home to me the shallowness of my commitment to Christ. I began to realise that I was prepared to allow Christ to affect my ideas – but not much else.

I know that many others have made that same discovery by thinking about the cross in this way. Knowing Christ crucified is one of the most astonishing privileges that we can hope to have. But we want to have it cheaply, on our own safe terms. Our old unredeemed natures fight a rearguard action, desperately trying to stop us from entering into the full and intimate relationship with Christ that will ultimately crucify and destroy them. A superficial knowledge of Christ allows our old nature to continue its existence, untroubled by the disturbing presence of Christ in our lives. It has often been said that the most characteristic effect of sin is delusion – the creating of the impression that all is well in our lives, and that no further action needs to be taken. This lie is exposed by the cross, which demands that we both appreciate its significance and apply it to our hearts.

I found this point brought out very helpfully in the writings of Johann Scheffler (1624–77), who wrote under the name of 'The Silesian Angel'. Scheffler stressed the need for a personally appropriated faith. The incarnation, crucifixion and resurrection must take place within me if they are to benefit me. Otherwise they would be external events which I had not taken into my life, allowing them to change me. The words that I found especially helpful go like this:

61 God must be born within you

Were Christ to be born a thousand times in Bethlehem,
And yet not be born in you, you will remain lost.

62 External things do not help

The cross of Golgotha cannot save you from sin,
Unless that cross is raised within you.

63 Raise yourself from the dead!

It does not help you that Christ is risen
If you remain bound to sin and death.[25]

After reading these words, I realised that I had kept the cross of Christ at a safe distance from me by insisting that I thought of it only in terms of historical events and theological concepts. Yet the words I had just read changed all that. The cross was not a distant event in history, whose relevance was limited to theological textbooks. It was a living reality which cried out for space in my life. I discovered, to my shame, that I had become very good at explaining the importance of the cross in the thought of Martin Luther or John Wesley, but had failed to see that the cross challenged me to become a new and better person. Like many others before me, I had become blind to the fact that the crucified Christ confronted me – not just others! – to fall down at its foot and try to start things all over again. It was profoundly helpful to me here to be able to draw on the experience of others who had made this discovery before me.

Yet the Christ who was crucified is also the one who has risen from the dead. It is therefore important to consider the implications of the resurrection for knowing Christ.

28

Knowing Christ as risen and ascended

The risen Christ is also the ascended Christ – the one who has conquered death, been publicly acclaimed as the Son of God and who now sits at the right hand of the Father. One of the great themes of the Christian life is that we shall one day reign in glory where Christ has gone before us. He has ascended into heaven to prepare a place for us, and eagerly awaits us to join him as his honoured guests. This powerful hope gives us great encouragement as we travel on the road of faith. Paul summarises the difference it should make to us as follows:

> So if you have been raised with Christ, seek the things that are above, where Christ is, seated at the right hand of God. Set your minds on things that are above, not on things that are on earth. For you have died, and your life is hidden with Christ in God.
>
> (Colossians 3:1–3)

Knowing Christ as ascended is to turn our eyes beyond the cares and concerns of this world and to recapture our vision of our final goal – the place to which our hearts are drawn, and to which we shall one day return in glory.

The New Testament is saturated with the news of a surprise – the astonishing declaration that the crucified Christ was raised to glory by God. Yet once people get used to a surprise, it stops being a surprise at all. Two thousand years of familiarity with this proclamation of resurrection have caused us to lose sight of the electrifying impact of the early Christian preaching. We have got used to the news of the resurrection. This familiarity has had its dreadful yet inevitable toll. What was once exciting and world-shattering has become ordinary and commonplace. So what can be done to recover this lost sense of wonder?

I began to get some helpful and satisfying answers when studying the writings of Martin Luther (1883–1546) during the period 1978–80. Luther invites us to read the Gospel accounts of the passion and death of Jesus, setting aside the knowledge that Jesus will rise again. By doing this, Luther believes that we will rediscover the hopelessness and helplessness of the first disciples after the crucifixion. We shall never be able to appreciate the joy of the resurrection until we have experienced the anguish and despair of the first disciples as they saw Christ suffer and die before their eyes. They had given up everything in order to follow Christ and had entrusted every aspect of their lives to him. Perhaps they expected him to be delivered from death; perhaps they expected an angel to intervene and take their Lord from the harsh cross and restore him to them. Yet as that first Good Friday unfolded, there was no sign of any intervention. Christ weakened, and finally died. Unless and until we appreciate the total despair experienced by those disciples, we shall never gain even the slightest insight into the joy brought by the resurrection.

I therefore began to read the passion narratives in a new way – or at least a way that was new for me. I tried to enter into the Gospel accounts of the suffering and death of Christ, using my imagination to build up a mental picture of what was taking place at Calvary. Like many people, in my reading of the passion narratives I had previously focused solely on the suffering of

Christ. The reason for this was simple: the more I appreciated what he suffered for me, the more I would gain an understanding of his love for me.

Now let me make it clear there is nothing wrong with this. It is a valid and authentic way of deepening our awareness of what Christ bore on that cross. We need to be made aware of all that he suffered on our behalf, partly to appreciate the costliness of our redemption and partly to appreciate how much our Saviour esteems those for whom he died. Yet by focusing *exclusively* on Christ, I had overlooked the impact that the cross was having on the disciples. They, too, were involved in what was going on. So I began to re-read these familiar passages, this time purposefully choosing to pay attention to what was happening to the followers of Jesus at this point. I therefore began to read the passion stories in a new light, focusing this time on the experiences of the disciples.

I found it helpful to focus on each of those present at the crucifixion, and to study their reactions. I discovered a band of bewildered people who were totally confused and demoralised by what was happening. Instead of trusting the promises of Christ in these dark moments, they abandoned him and placed their trust in their own perceptions of the situation. God seemed to be absent, and all seemed to be lost. They were in utter despair. In each case, the reaction was entirely understandable from a human point of view. If I had been there, I would have done the same. It is so easy to judge those disciples as if we would have behaved better or known better. Yet the harsh reality is that we would have done the same. They had lost all that they cherished, all that they had based their lives upon. They knew that they had to build their lives upon a rock rather than shifting sand. Christ seem to them to be that rock, and they had built their houses of faith upon that foundation. And now that foundation seemed to have collapsed and been destroyed. Everything they had trusted and valued seemed to have been taken away from them. It seemed they had nothing left.

Having entered into the hopeless and helpless situation of the disciples, I found the resurrection narratives to be charged with personal and spiritual significance. It was not simply that Christ was risen from the dead, nor that the resurrection demonstrated Jesus to be the Son of God. It was also that the despair and hopelessness experienced by those disciples on that first Good Friday were overturned. Not only had Christ been restored to them; the promises of God had been demonstrated to be completely trustworthy, even when everything seemed to suggest they were not. The resurrection of Christ offers us the most powerful reminder and reassurance that we may trust God, even when everything around us is collapsing and we are unable to discern God's presence anywhere.

To know Christ is to know the total reliability of a loving and caring God, even when everything in our experience seems to point in the opposite direction. We see so much in the world that perplexes us and causes us to doubt. How can there be a God when there is so much suffering in the world? How can the resurrection be a victory over sin and death, when sin continues to be a living presence in the life of the believer and death remains the grim finality which confronts us? It is very easy for us to identify with those perplexed and agonised disciples, as the dead body of their Lord was taken down from the cross and taken away for burial. We need to hold fast to the promises of God to be with us, even when we walk in the valley of the shadow of death. There will be times when we cannot sense his presence, and when everything around us seems to proclaim his absence.

It is at those moments that the full meaning of the resurrection of Christ is to be grasped. To know Christ as the one who has been crucified and has risen is to find comfort in the knowledge of the presence of God in moments of despair and anguish – moments when we feel profoundly alone, abandoned and without any helper.

The lesson these reflections prompted was my profound need

to trust God. In the past, I often trusted God because my experience pointed in that direction, because I felt good, or because things seemed to be going well in the world. Thinking about the resurrection of Christ helped me to realise that the only secure ground of trust in God is the total reliability of God himself, at all times and in all places – and that Christ is the one who makes this total reliability known.

So what are the implications of this for knowing Christ? Perhaps the greatest is also the simplest: that while we can never hope to prove conclusively that the gospel is true, we can nevertheless trust totally in the reliability of God. So many people long for certainty and find themselves totally perplexed when they cannot prove the truth of the gospel to their friends, or even to themselves. Yet the gospel is not primarily about a set of ideas whose truth can be proved before the court of reason. The gospel is relational. It concerns a personal trans-forming encounter with the living God, who is made known and available to us through Christ. And in relationships, the absolutely critical thing is the total trustworthiness of the person we come to know and love. In the end, the critical questions we must ask in such circumstances are these. Is this someone we can rely on totally, even in life's darkest and most difficult moments? Is this someone we can depend upon, even when everyone else abandons us?

I found that I needed to know Christ as the anchor which gave me stability in life's stormy seas, as the rock on which I could build my house of faith, knowing that it can survive the buffeting of wind and rain. I needed to go beyond knowing *that* Christ was an anchor; I needed to *experience* him as my anchor in the stormy seas of life. To know Christ and the power of his resurrection (Philippians 3:10) is to be able to face life's many dangers, challenges and fears, knowing *as a lived reality* – and not just as an *idea* – that nothing can separate us from his presence and love (Romans 8:31–9). Yes, there is far more to the risen Christ than such assurances. Yet these give our walk of faith the stability and confidence that we need if we are to complete the journey of faith.

Christianity is a religion of hope, which focuses on the resurrection and ascension of Christ as the grounds for believing and trusting in a God who is able to triumph over death, give hope to all those who suffer and die, and finally gather believers together in the New Jerusalem. Something which happened in the past – Christ's death and resurrection – has thus inaugurated something new, which will reach its final consummation in the future. The Christian believer is caught up in this tension between the 'now' and the 'not yet'. In one sense, heaven has not yet happened; in another, its powerful lure already impacts upon us in a dramatic and complex fashion, in which we are at one and the same time excited at the prospect of finally entering its portals, and yet are dejected through knowing that we are not there yet.

The term 'heaven' is used frequently in the Pauline writings of the New Testament to refer to the Christian hope. Although it is natural to think of heaven as a future entity, Paul's thinking appears to embrace both a future reality and a spiritual sphere or realm which co-exists with the material world of space and time. Thus, 'heaven' is referred to both as the future home of the believer (2 Corinthians 5:1–2; Philippians 3:20) and as the present dwelling-place of Jesus Christ, from which he will come in final judgement (Romans 10:6; 1 Thessalonians 1:10; 4:16).

One of Paul's most significant statements concerning heaven focuses on the notion of believers being 'citizens of heaven' (Philippians 3:20), and in some way sharing in the life of heaven in the present. The tension between the 'now' and the 'not yet' is evident in Paul's writings on this theme, making it very difficult to sustain the simple idea of heaven as something which will not come into being until the future or which cannot be experienced in the present.

Probably the most helpful way of thinking of heaven is as a

consummation of the Christian doctrine of salvation, in which the presence, penalty and power of sin have been finally eliminated and the total presence of God in individuals and the community of faith has been achieved. No obstacle now remains to separate us from Christ. It should be noted that the New Testament parables of heaven are strongly communal in nature – for example, heaven is portrayed as a banquet, a wedding feast or a city, the new Jerusalem. Individualist interpretations of heaven or eternal life are also excluded on account of the Christian understanding of God as Trinity. Eternal life is thus not a projection of an individual human existence, but is rather to be seen as sharing, with the redeemed community as a whole, in the community of a loving God.

The theme of the hope of heaven, and especially the consummation of all things in the heavenly Jerusalem, is of major importance in Christian spirituality. In the medieval period, the Latin term *viator* (literally, a 'wayfarer') was used to refer to the believer, who was envisaged as a pilgrim travelling to the heavenly city. The vision of the heavenly city was seen as an encouragement and inspiration to those engaged on this pilgrimage. Many writings of the period direct the believer to focus attention on the glorious hope of final entry into the New Jerusalem, and the rejoicing and delight which this will bring. Such thoughts were widely regarded as an encouragement, enabling believers to deal with the disappointments and hardships which were so often their lot. Much the same theme can, of course, be found in other types of spirituality, such as John Bunyan's famous allegory *The Pilgrim's Progress* (1678).

It was this aspect of the Christian faith which attracted such severe criticism from Karl Marx (1818–83). Marx regarded religion as the 'opiate of the people' partly on account of the strongly positive vision set out by Christianity for the future life, which enabled Christians to cope with hardship, suffering and deprivation in the light of the hope that was set before them. For Marx, this hope deflected them from attending to issues of worldly importance, such as the alleviation of poverty and attending to issues of social justice.

The theme of the Christian hope can also be stated in terms of catching a glimpse of the Promised Land – seen, as with Moses, from the mountain peak across the Jordan – and finally entering into it. This is demonstrated in many of the sermons of the great African-American civil rights leader Martin Luther King (1929–68), who also shows clearly how the theme of the Christian hope can be linked with a call to political action. King's final sermon was delivered on 3 April 1968 at the Mason Temple in Memphis, Tennessee (the headquarters of the largest African-American Pentecostal denomination in the United States). The sermon is saturated with calls to action, coupled with a strong affirmation of the importance of hope in the future, linked with the imagery of the Promised Land. It ends as follows:

> We've got some difficult days ahead. But it doesn't matter with me now. Because I've been to the mountaintop. And I don't mind. Like anybody, I would like to live a long life. Longevity has its place. But I'm not concerned about that now. I just want to do God's will. And he's allowed me to go up to the mountain. And I've looked over. And I've seen the Promised Land. I may not get there with you. But I want you to know tonight that we, as a people, will get to the Promised Land. And I'm happy, tonight. I'm not worried about anything. I'm not fearing any man. Mine eyes have seen the glory of the coming of the Lord.[26]

Perhaps this is a fitting point at which to bring this work to an end. We journey in hope, looking forward to that final day on which we will stand in Christ's presence. In the meantime, we are sustained and encouraged by that sense of anticipation. The Promised Land lies ahead, and one day we shall enter and possess it. We can distantly hear the music of its merrymaking and see the light of its citadel. Each day that we travel brings us nearer to our spiritual homeland, and to the Christ who we long to know more fully.

It is one thing to *believe* in the hope of heaven; it is, however, quite another to *sustain* that hope and allow it to saturate our thoughts and aspirations. We need to do more than understand the teaching of the New Testament on this matter. We must allow this hope to nourish and sustain us, to infect us with its joy and wonder – and to make us long to be in that place where, one day, we shall rest in peace, knowing Christ fully and luxuriating in his presence.

Notes

Sources of major citations are here provided. For additional texts and discussion, see Alister E. McGrath, *Christian Spirituality: An Introduction* (Oxford: Blackwell, 1999).

1 Francis de Sales, *Introduction à la vie dévoté* (Paris: Mame-Tours, 1939), 89.
2 Leonardo Boff, *Trinity and Society* (London: Burns & Oates, 1988), 159.
3 Ludolf of Saxony, *Vita Jesu Christi Domini ac salvatoris nostri* (Paris: U. Gering & B. Rembolt, 1502), preface.
4 Gerard of Zutphen, *The Spiritual Ascent* (London: Burns & Oates, 1908), 26.
5 Isaac Watts, 'When I survey the wondrous cross'. Sources of hymns have not been provided, given the extensive range of hymnals readily available. There are also a number of websites dedicated to hymns, including http://www.hymnsite.com and http://www.ccel.org/cceh.
6 *The Journal of the Revd John Wesley*, 8 vols (London: Culley, 1909–16), vol. 1, 475–6.

7   Ignatius Loyola, *Spiritual Exercises*, 47–8; in *Obras Completas*, 2nd edn (Madrid: Biblioteca de autores cristianos, 1963), 209–10.

8   George Herbert, 'Love III', in *The Works of George Herbert*, ed. F. E. Hutchinson (Oxford: Clarendon Press, 1941), 188–9.

9   J. R. W. Stott, *I Believe in Preaching* (London: Hodder & Stoughton, 1982), 202–3.

10 Martin Luther, 'Sermons on the Gospel of John', in *D. Martin Luthers Werke: Kritisch Gesamtausgabe*, vol. 45 (Weimar: Böhlau, 1938), 498–9.

11 Horatius Bonar, *When God's Children Suffer* (New Canaan, CT: Keats Publishing, 1981), 121.

12 Jean Pierre de Caussade, *L'abandon à la providence divine* (Paris: Desclée de Brouwer, 1966), 23.

13 Charlotte Elliot, 'O Lamb of God, I come'.

14 Horatio G. Spafford, 'It is well with my soul'.

15 Martin Luther, 'The great catechism', exposition of the second article, in *Die Bekenntisschriften der evangelisch-lutherischen Kirche*, 2nd edn (Göttingen: Vandenhoeck & Ruprecht, 1952), 652. (Translation of German text.)

16 Bernard of Clairvaux, 'Jesus, Thou Joy of loving hearts'.

17 Charles Wesley, 'And can it be?' This hymn is also known as 'Free grace'.

18 Martin Luther, 'The great catechism', exposition of the first commandment, in *Die Bekenntisschriften der evangelisch-lutherischen Kirche*, 2nd edn (Göttingen: Vandenhoeck & Ruprecht, 1952), 560. (Translation of German text.)

19 Bernard of Clairvaux (attrib.), 'O sacred head, sore wounded'.

20 *The Prayers and Meditations of St Anselm* (Harmondsworth: Penguin Books, 1973), 94.

21 Bernard of Clairvaux, *de diligendo Deo*, 4.

22 St Patrick, 'The deer's cry', also known as 'St Patrick's breastplate'.

23 Mrs Cecil F. Alexander, 'Once in royal David's city'.

24 Ignatius Loyola, *Spiritual Exercises*, 47–8, in *Obras Completas*,

2nd edn (Madrid: Biblioteca de autores cristianos, 1963), 211.

25 Angelus Silesius, *Der cherubinischer Wandersmann*, I.61–3, in *Sämtliche poetische Werke*. 3 vols (Munich: Allgemeine Verlagsanstalt, 1924), vol. 3, 19–20.

26 Martin Luther King, 'I see the Promised Land', in *Martin Luther King: A Documentary*, ed. Flip Schulke (New York: Norton, 1976), 223.

Also by Alister McGrath:

In the Beginning
The Story of the King James Bible

The King James Bible was a landmark in the history of the
English language, and an inspiration to poets, dramatists, artists
and politicians. Without the King James Bible there would
have been no *Paradise Lost*, no *Pilgrim's Progress*, no Handel's
Messiah, no Negro spirituals, no Gettysburg address. The
culture of the English-speaking world would have been
immeasurably impoverished.

Yet as well as being a literary and religious classic, the King
James Bible was also seen as a social, economic and political
text. Those seeking to overthrow the English monarch and
those wishing to retain it both sought support from the
same Bible. The Bible came to be seen as the foundation
of every aspect of English culture, linking monarch
and church, time and eternity.

So how did this remarkable translation come to be written?
In the Beginning tells the extraordinary tale, set against the
backdrop of the tumultuous century of events which
brought it into being.

Published by Hodder & Stoughton
ISBN 0 340 78585 3

The Journey
A Pilgrim in the Lands of the Spirit

*'A golden book on the Christian life, guaranteed
to excite, encourage and energise.'*
J. I. PACKER

The Christian faith is like a journey. At times it is enormously
exciting and rewarding. At others it is wearying and
discouraging. So what can we do? This book offers
answers. Above all, it encourages us to take courage from
others who have travelled before us.

Alister McGrath is our guide on an epic journey that retraces
the path of the great Exodus from Egypt. Through the
wilderness and over the mountains, he helps us to address a
series of spiritual obstacles – doubt, distraction, temptation,
tiredness, emptiness and low self-esteem – by introducing us
to fellow travellers met along the way: giants of Christian
spirituality, including C.S. Lewis, J.I. Packer and John Bunyan.

The Journey is the perfect introduction to authentic
Christian spirituality, showing us how we can deepen our
relationship with God by following in the footsteps of
the classic Christian writers.

Published by Hodder & Stoughton
ISBN 0 340 73533 3